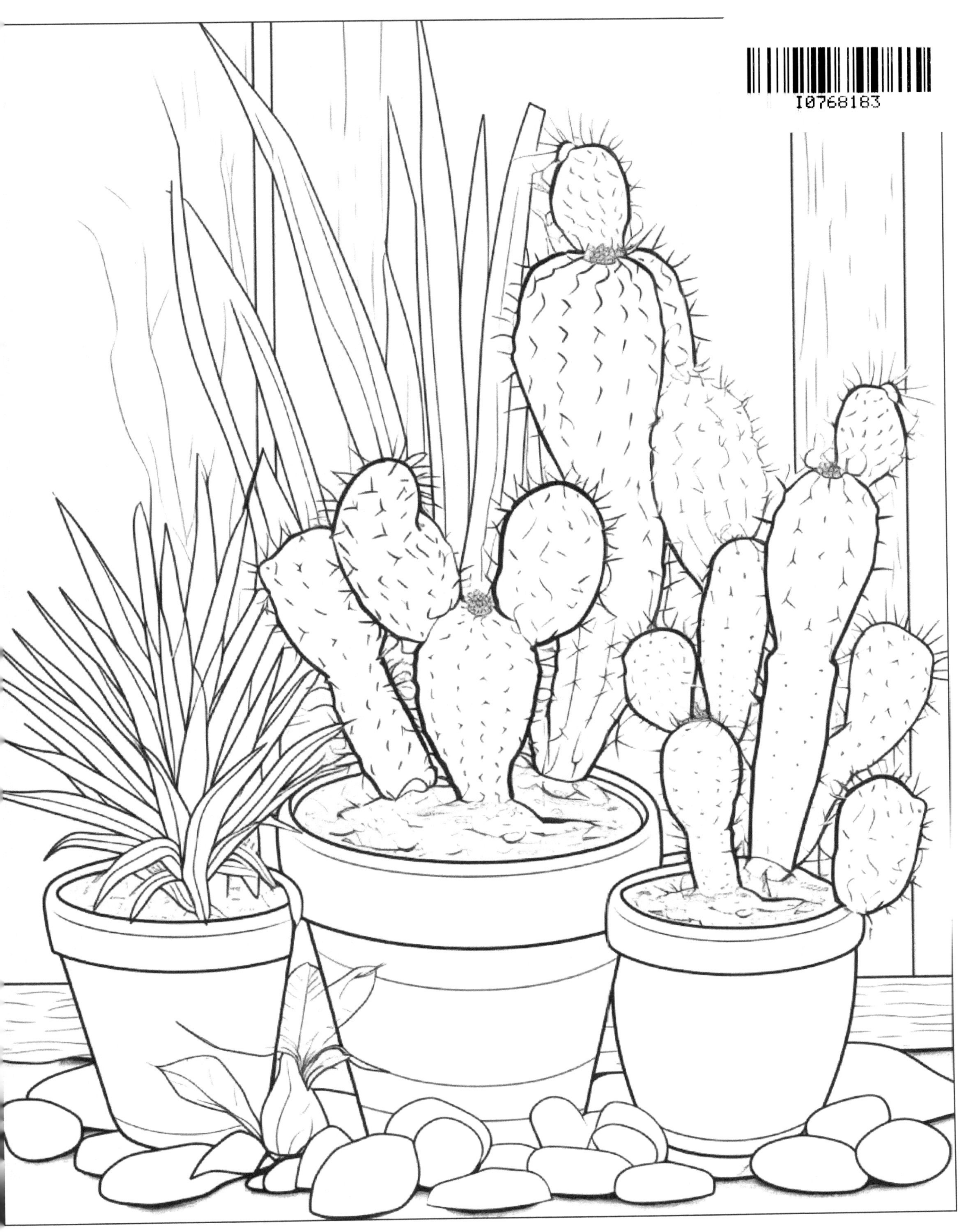
I0768183

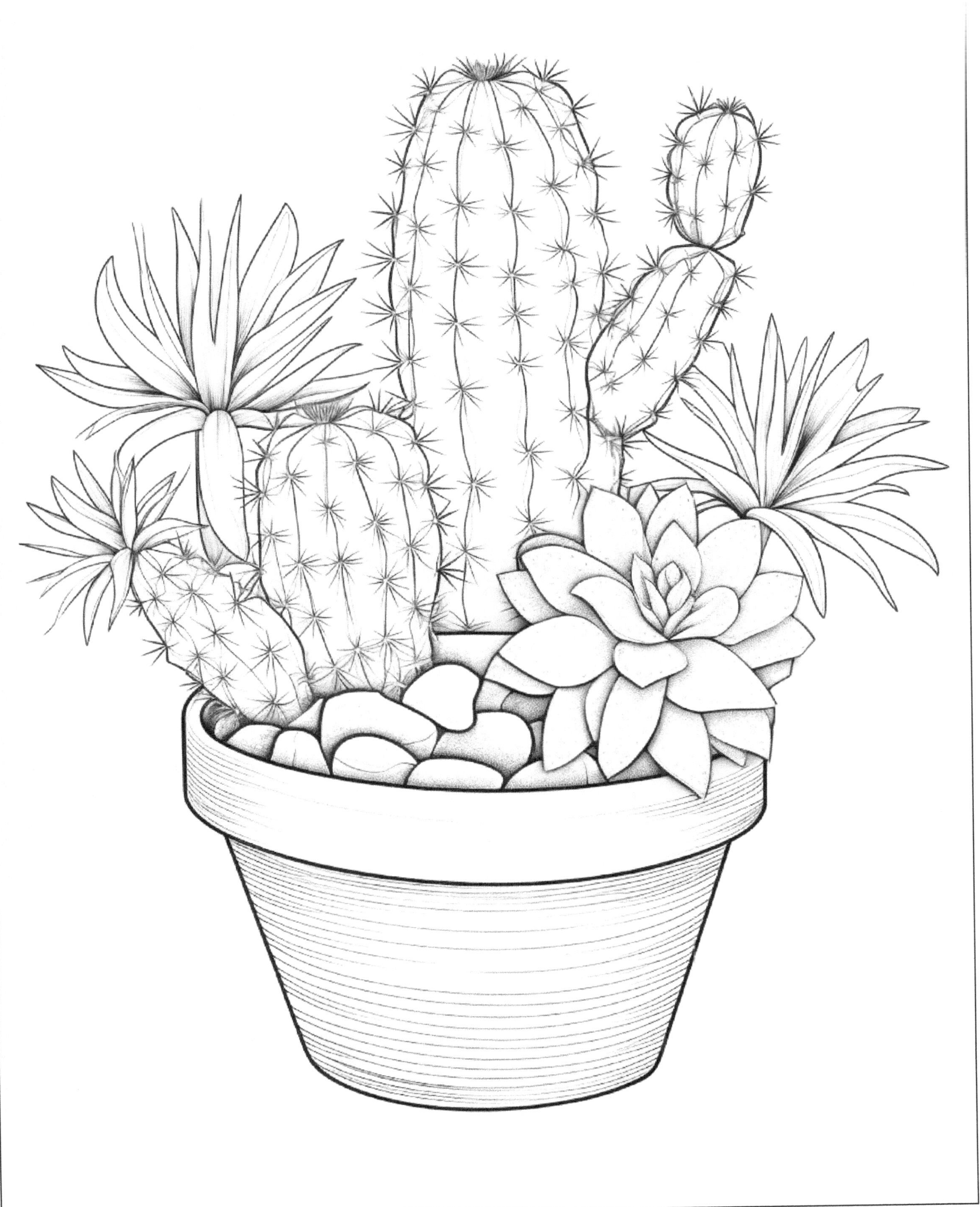

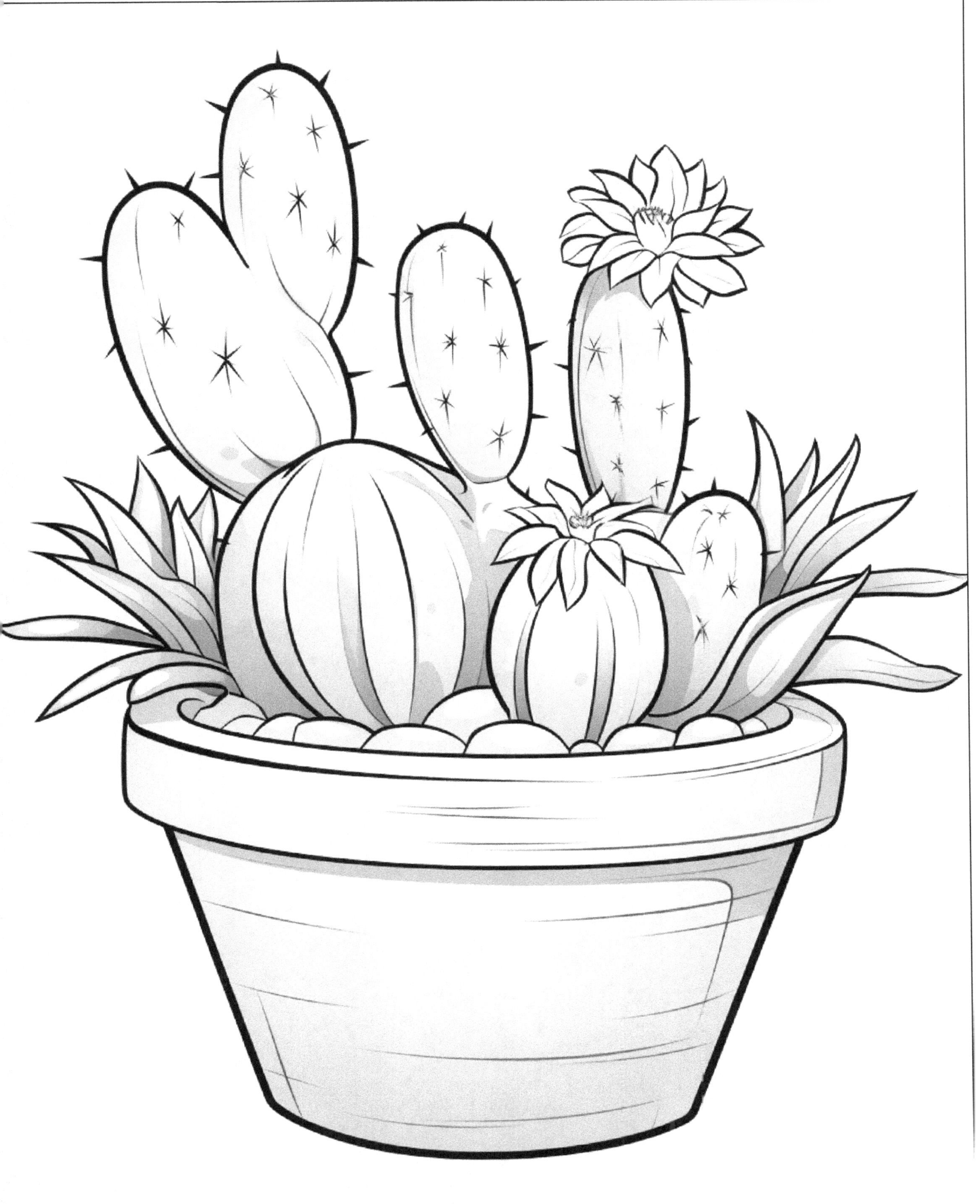

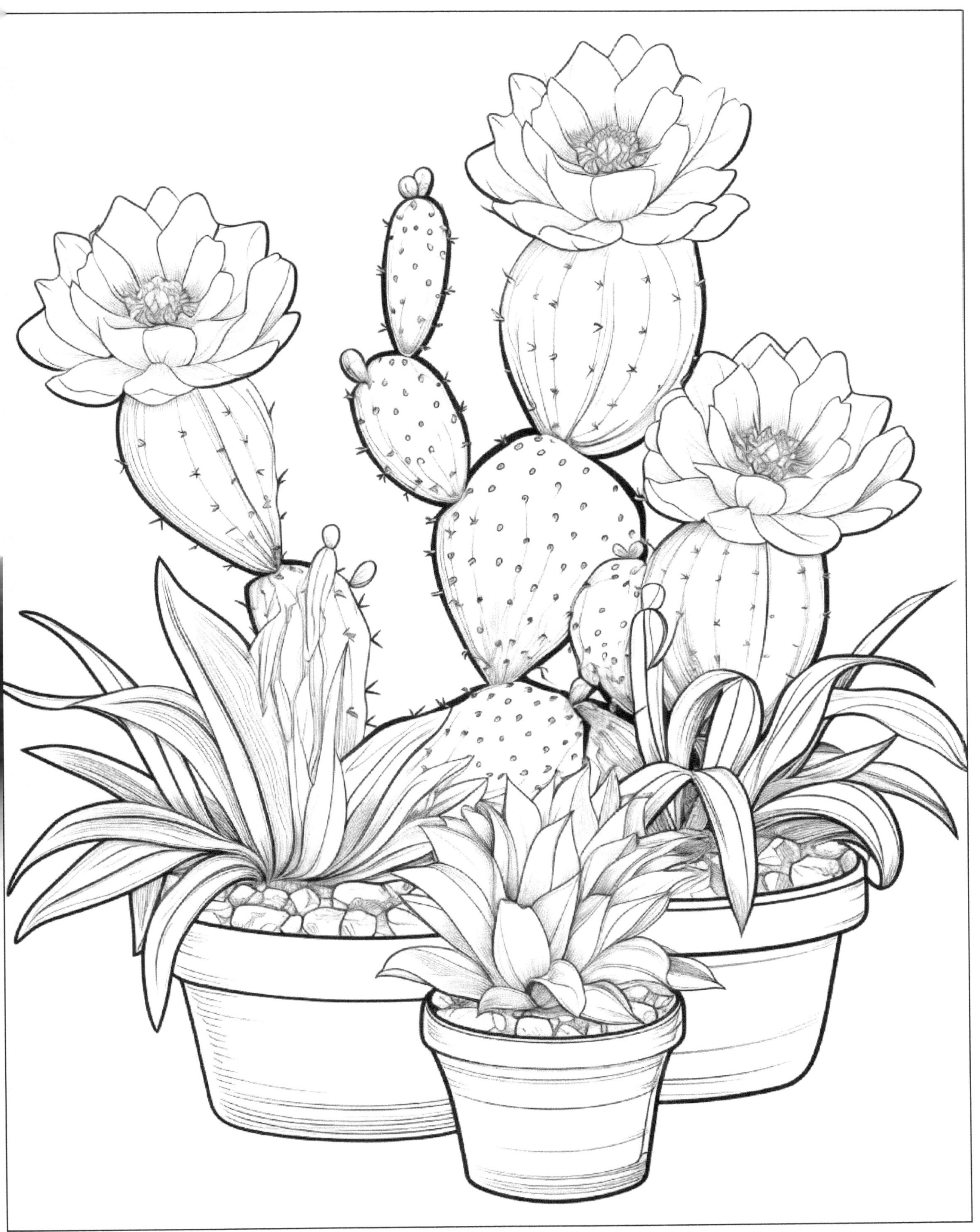

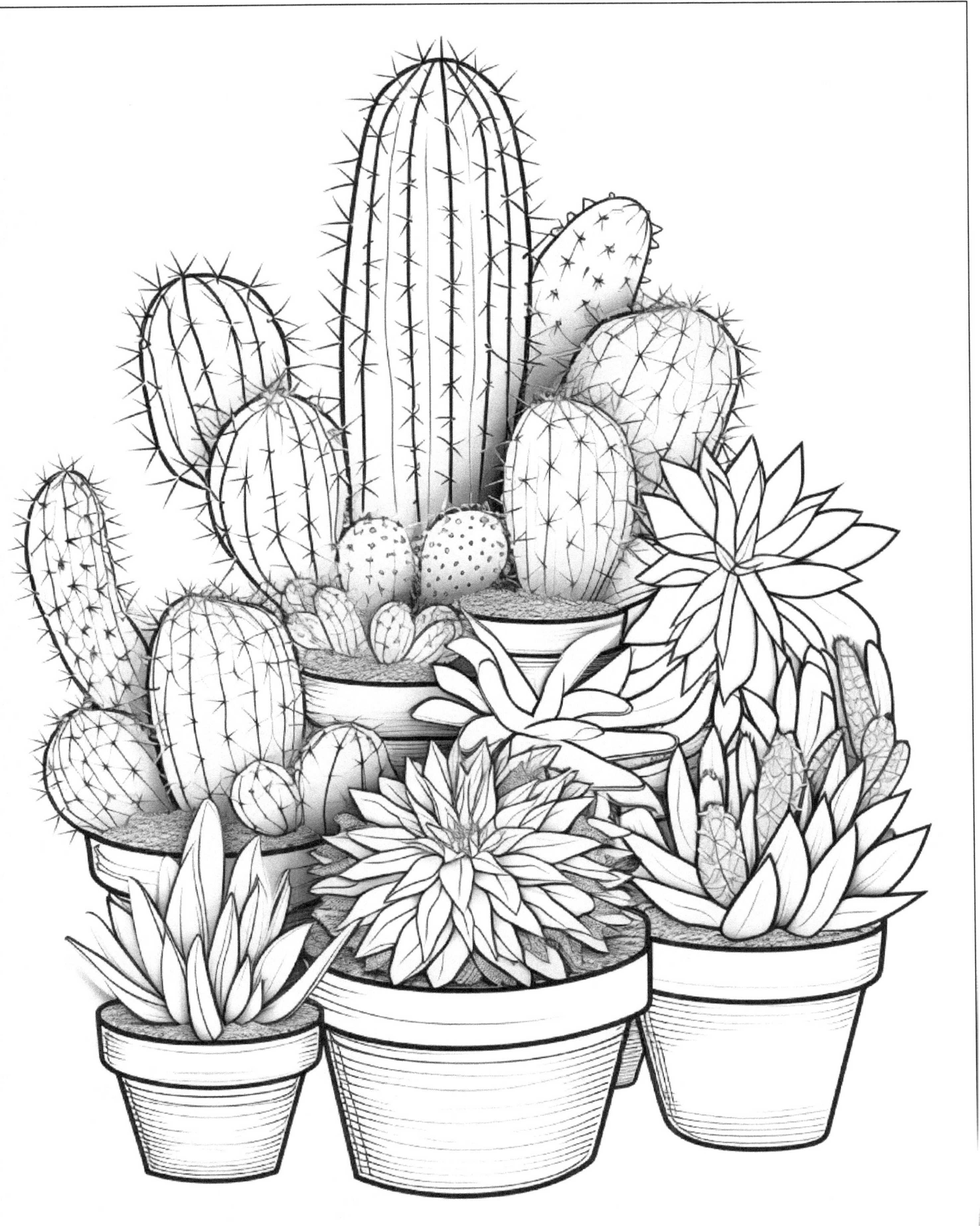

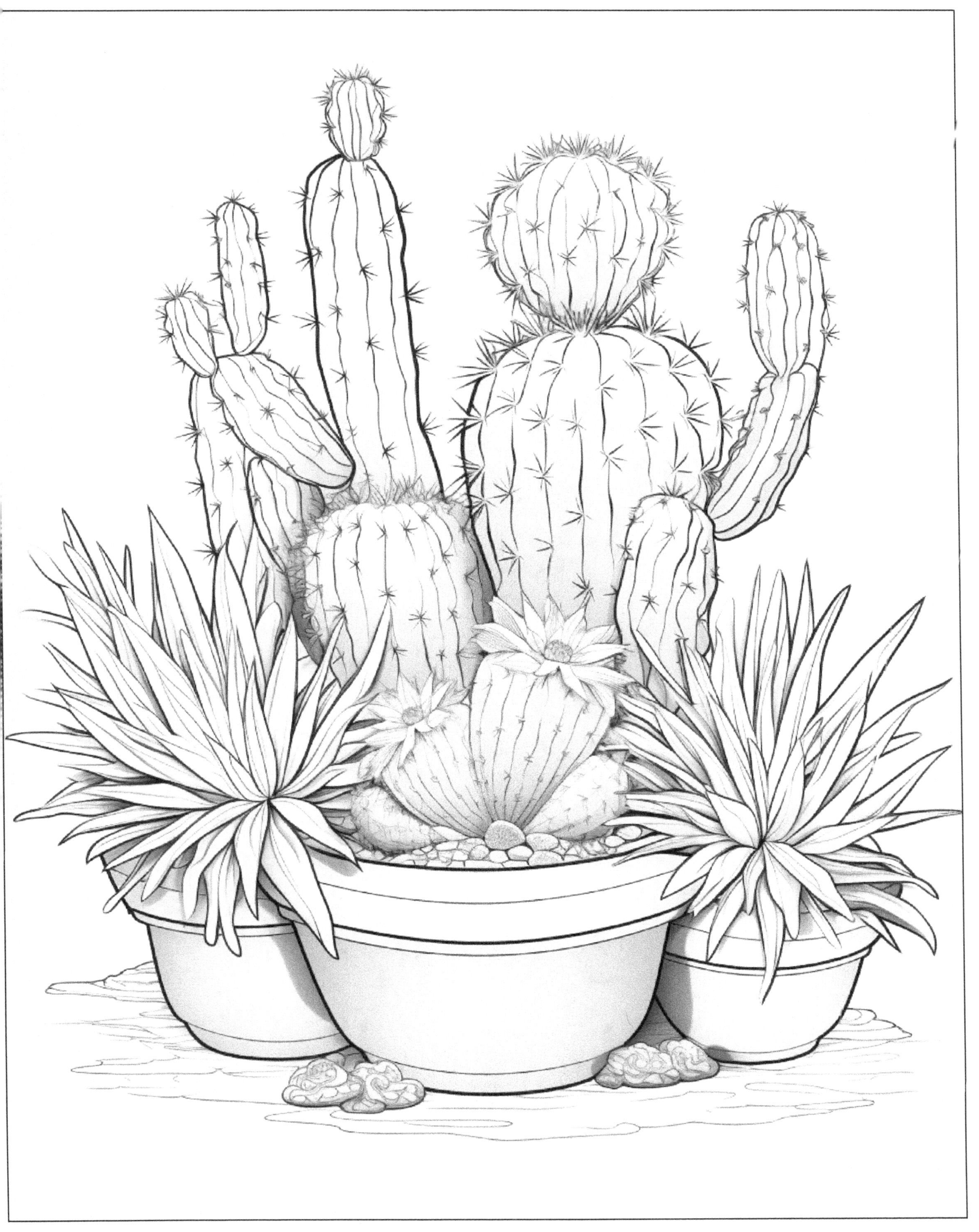

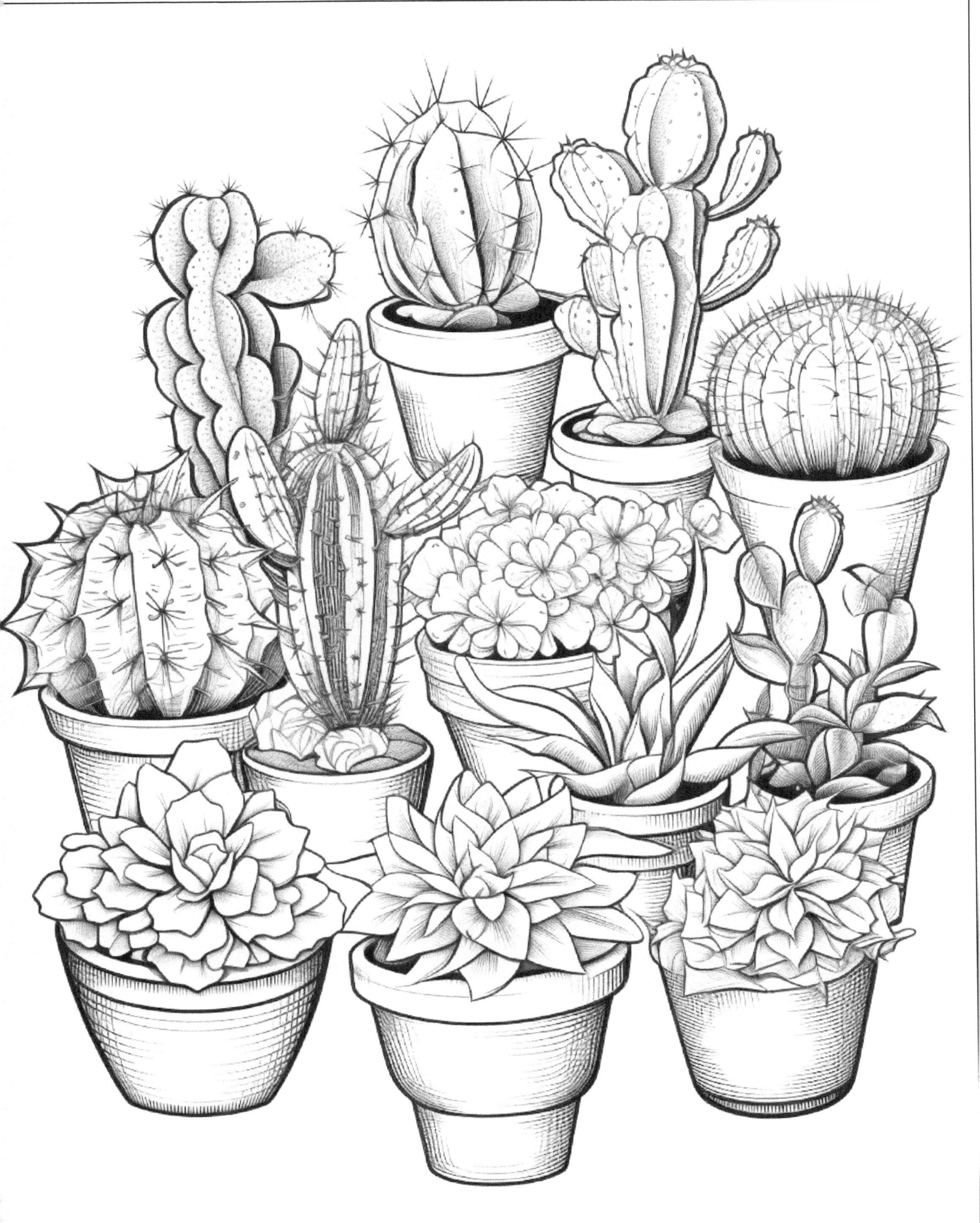

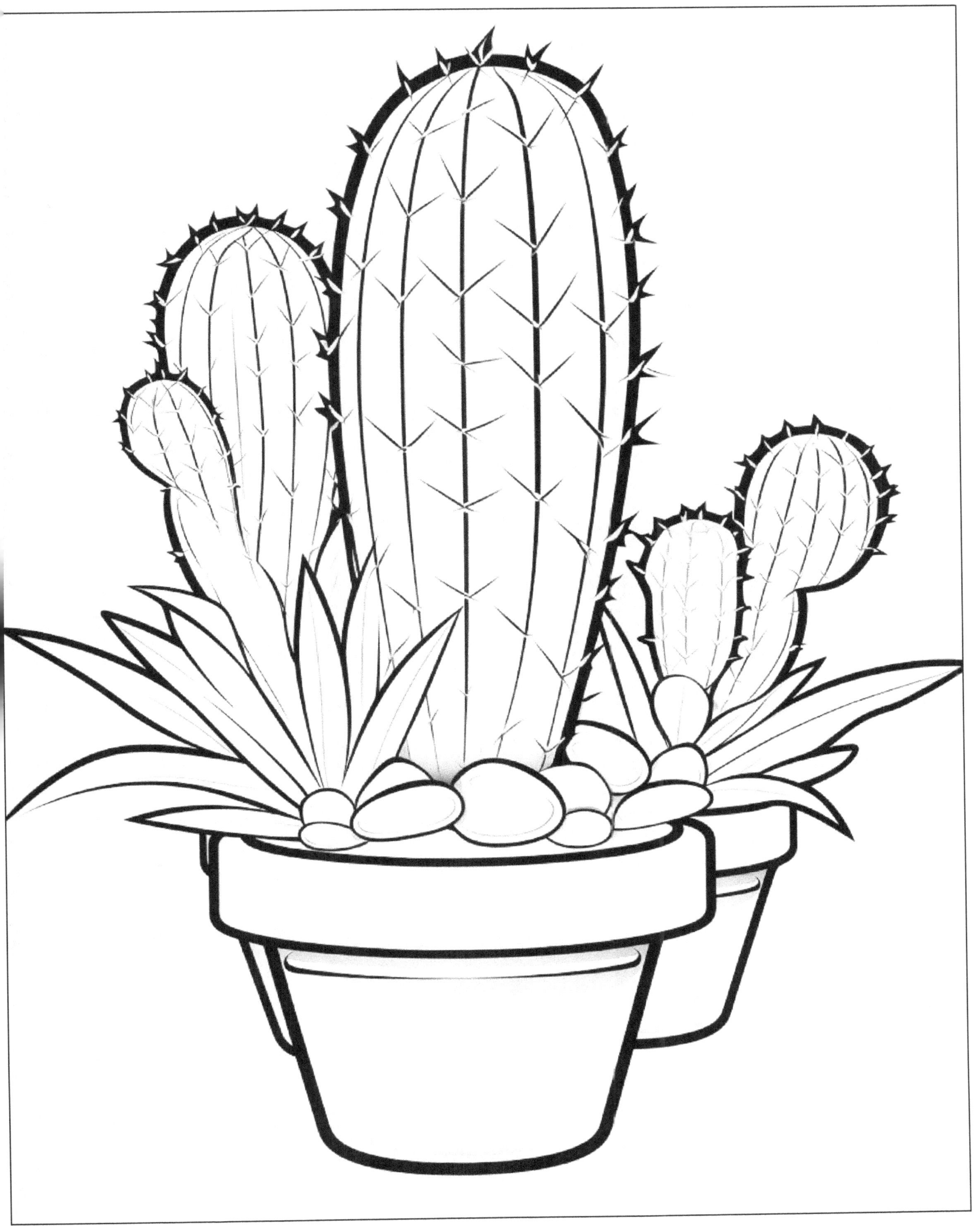

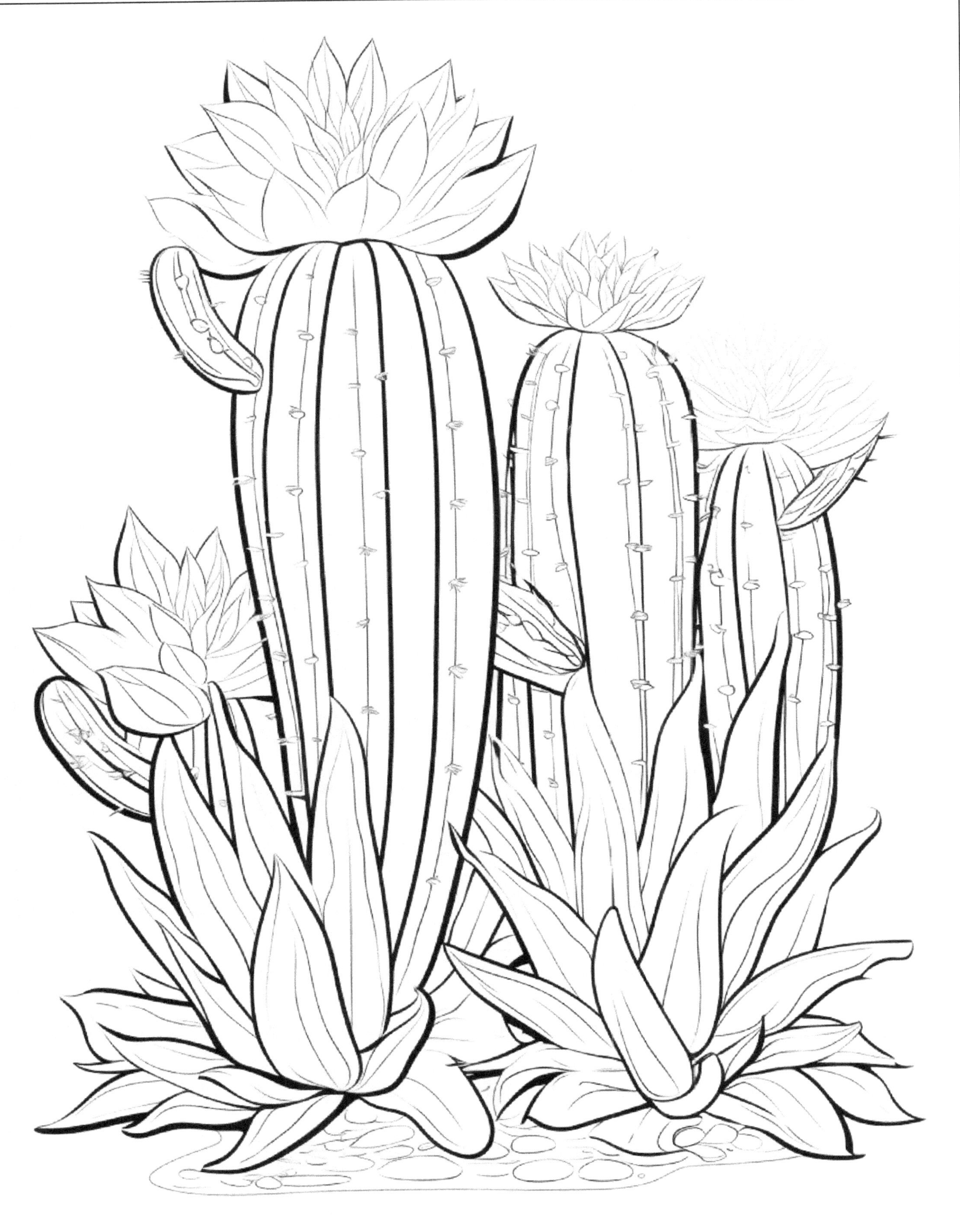

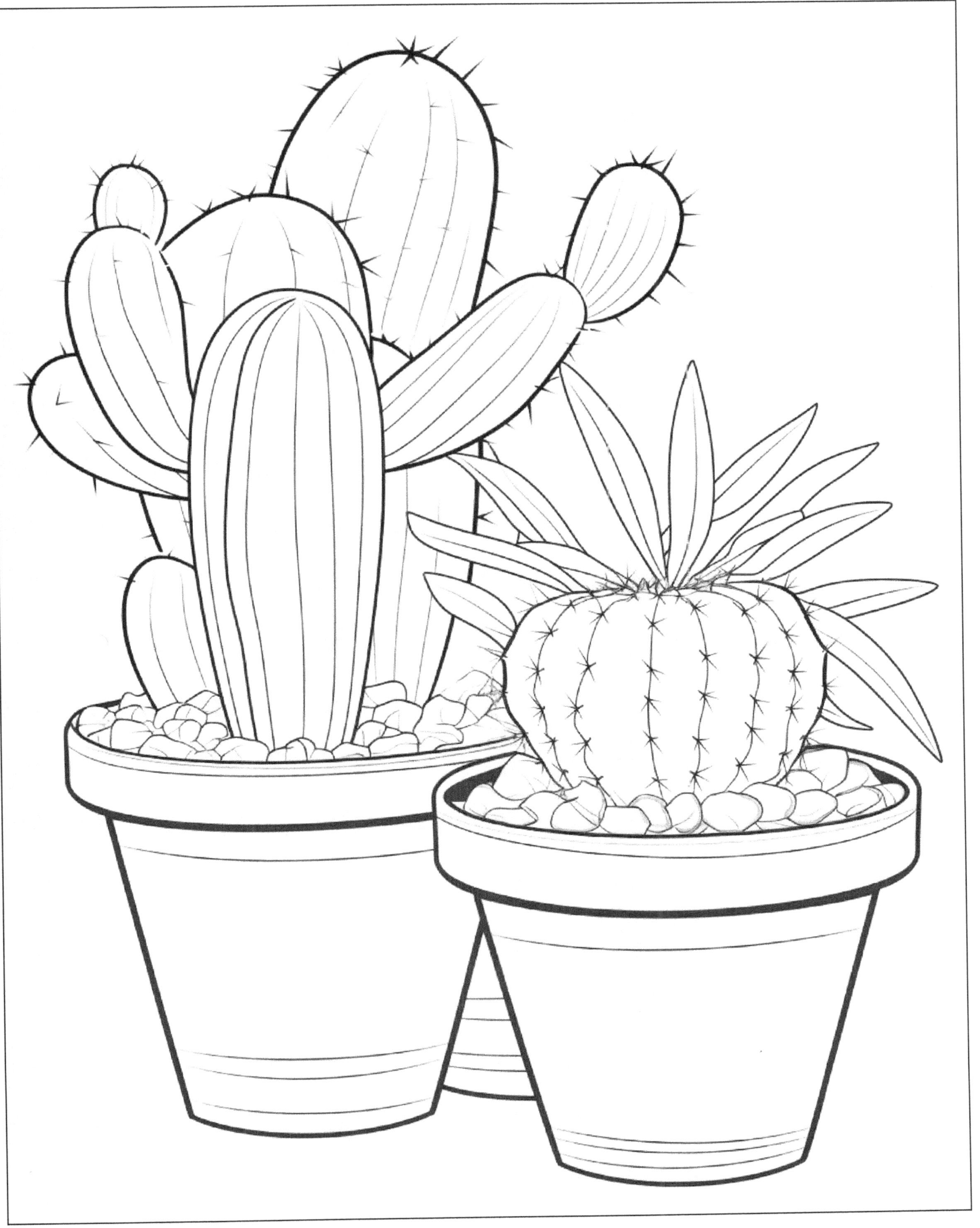

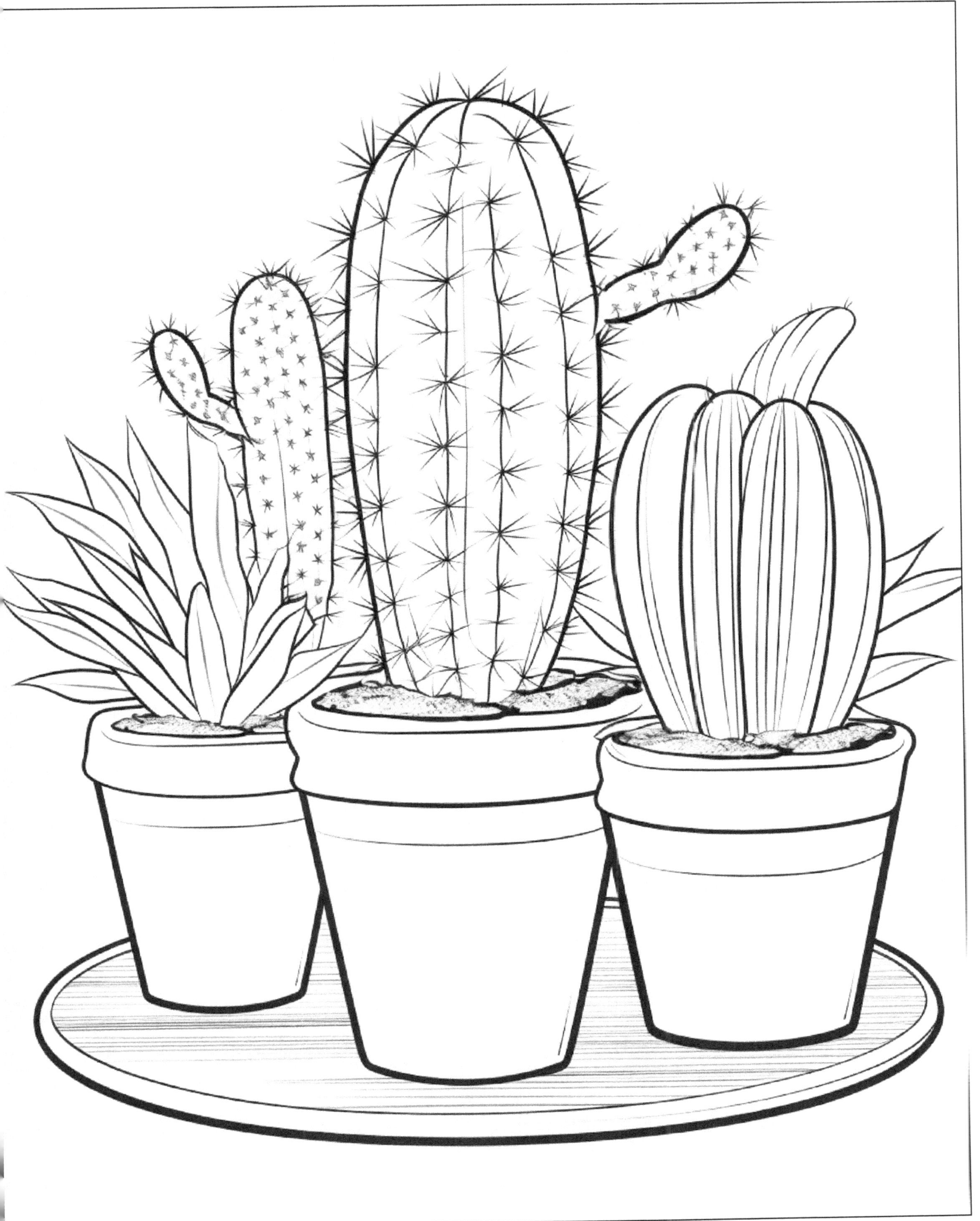

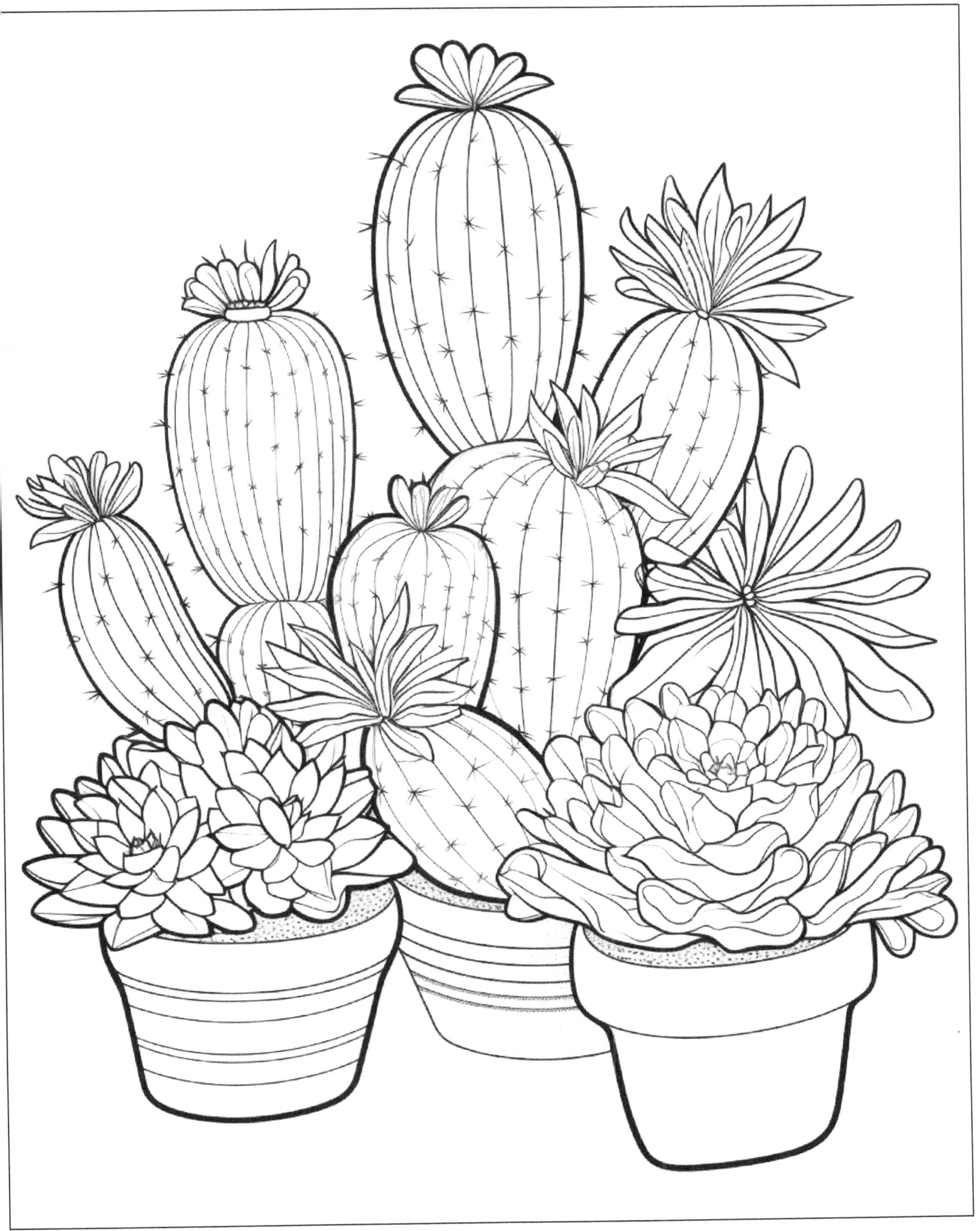

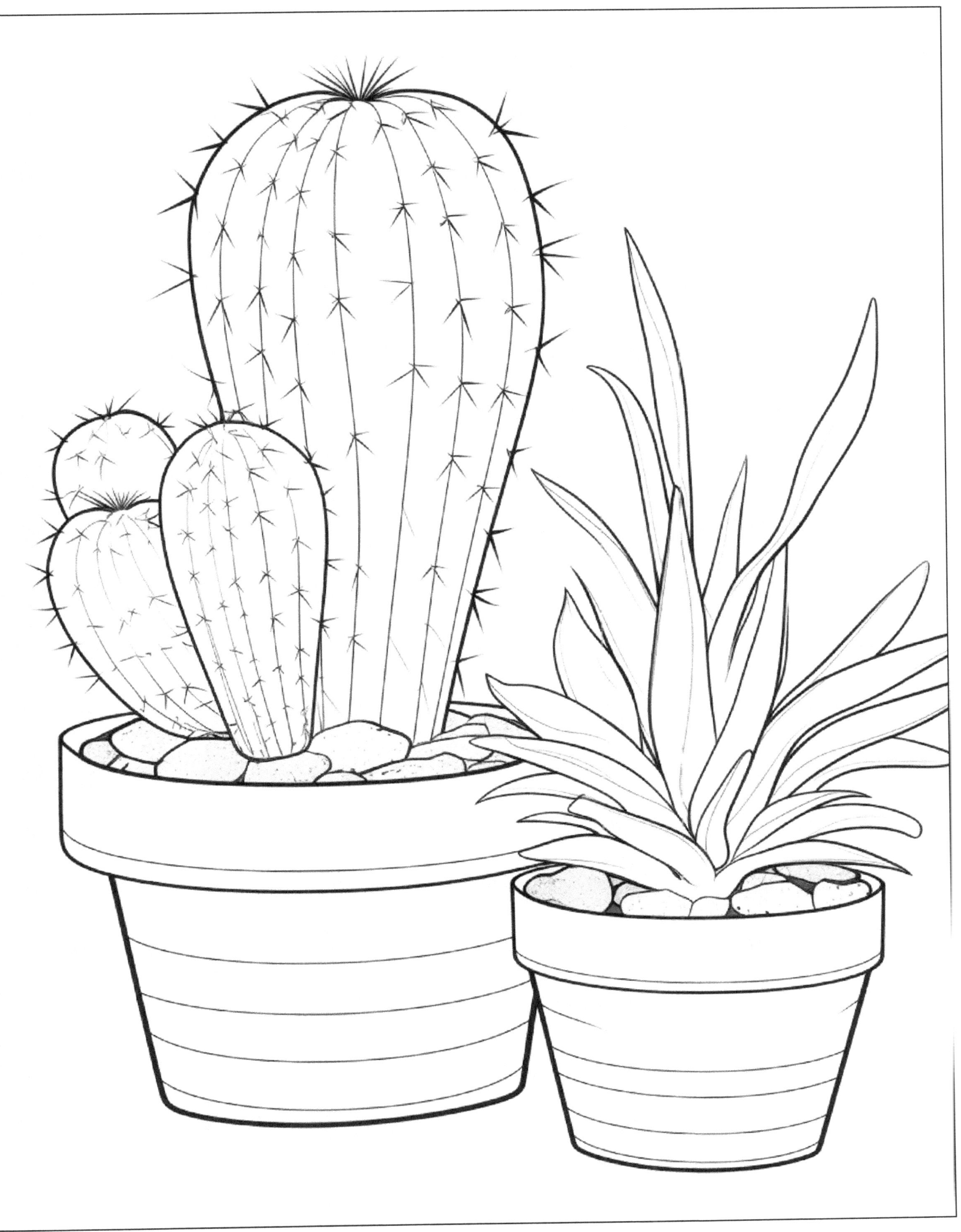

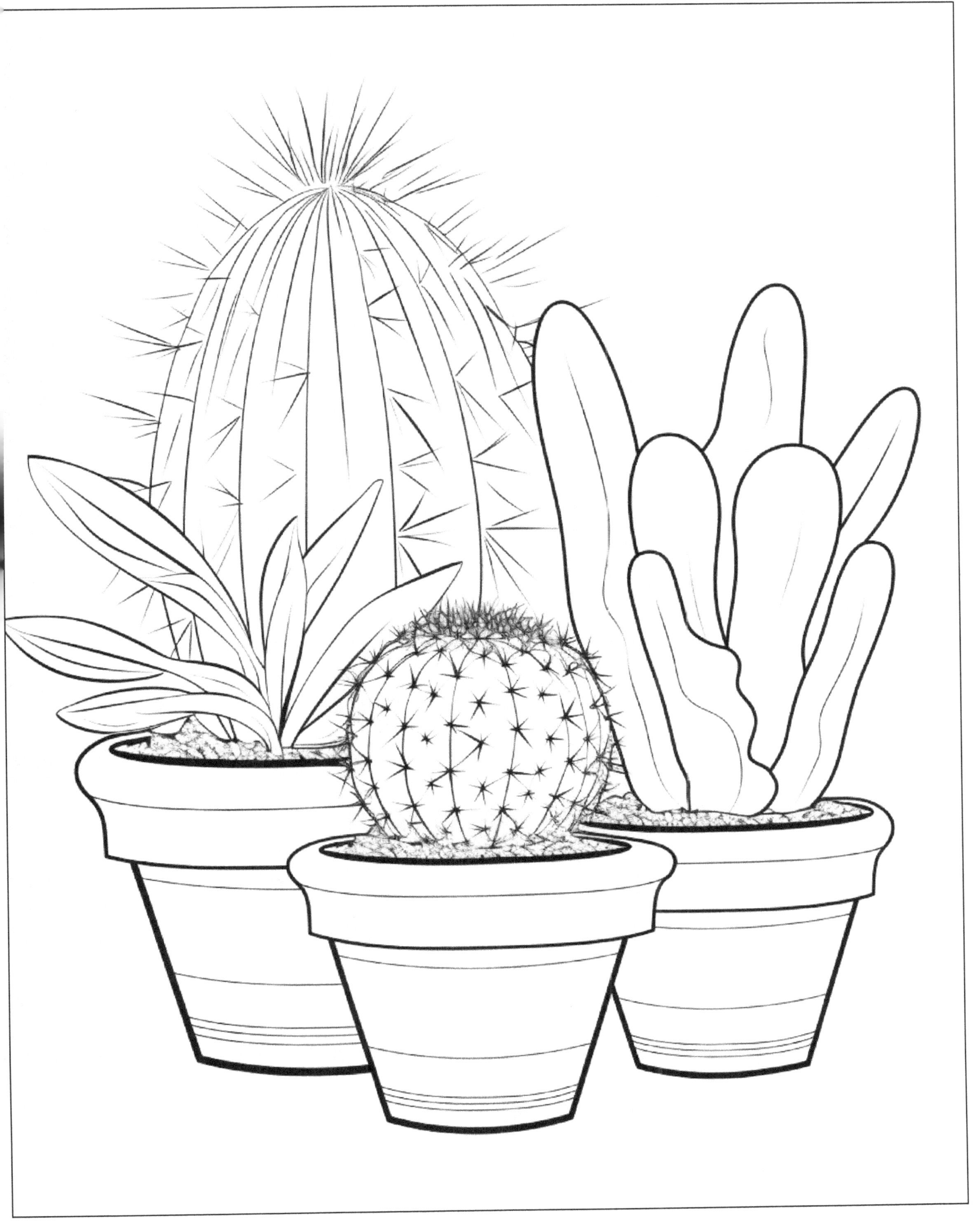

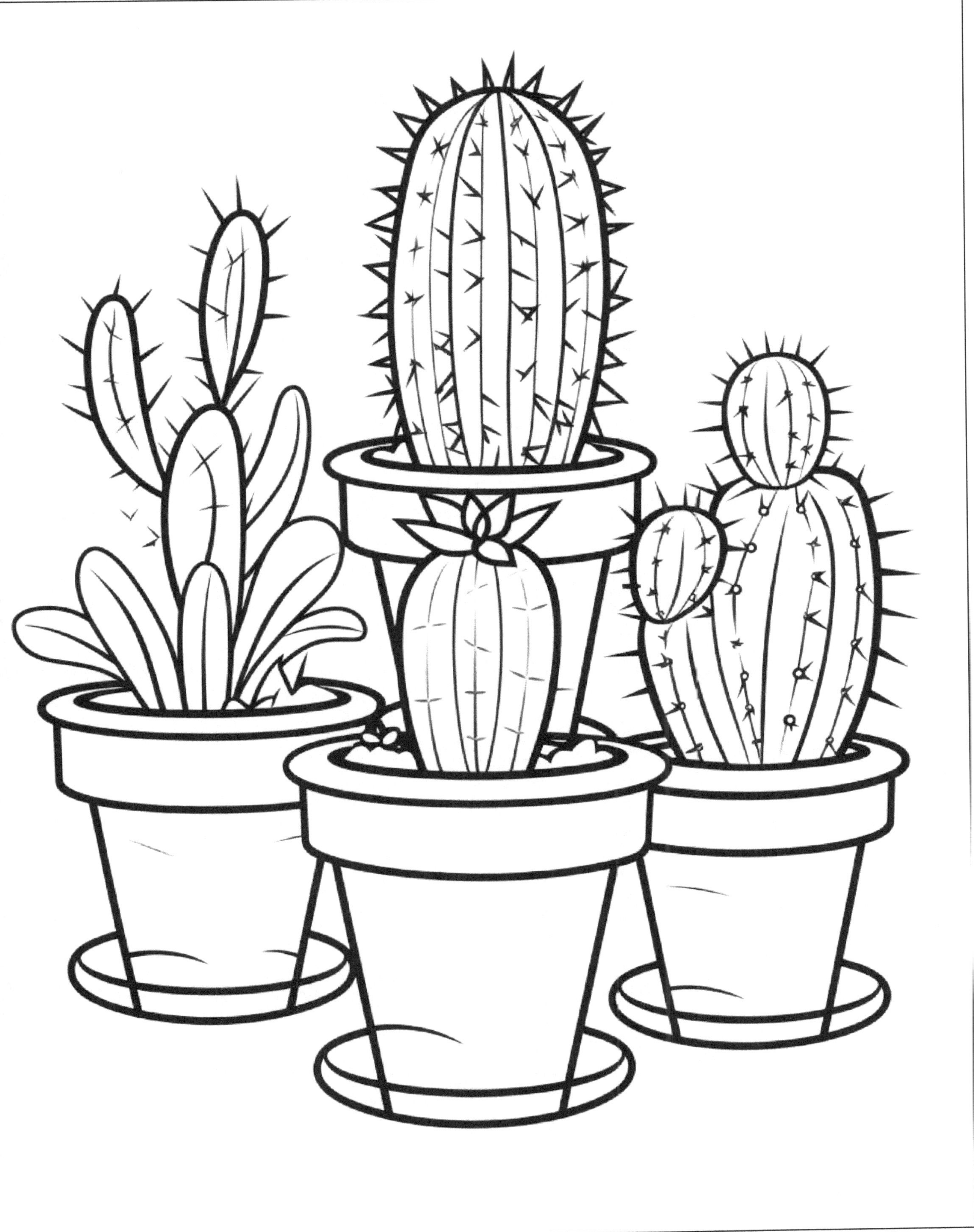

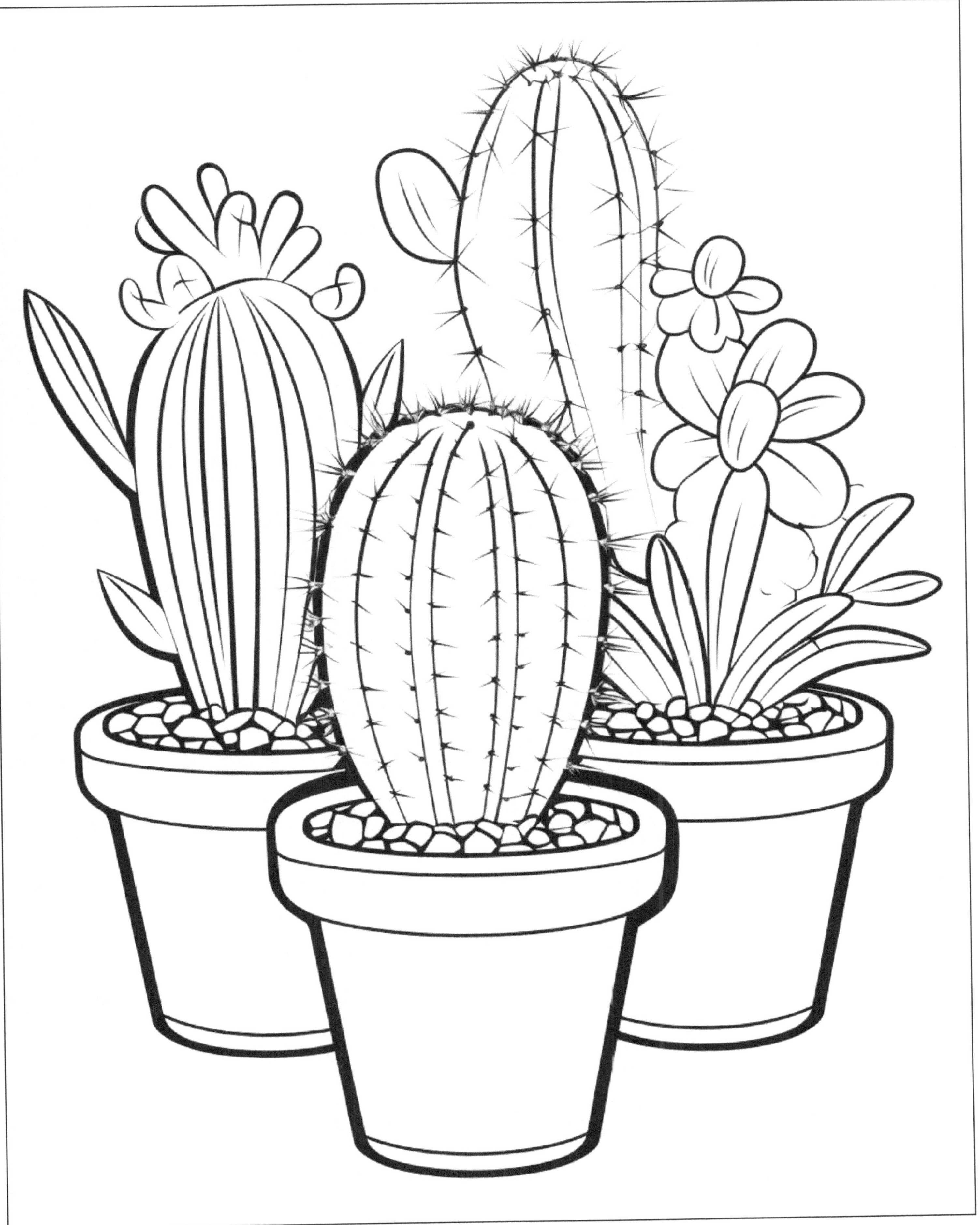

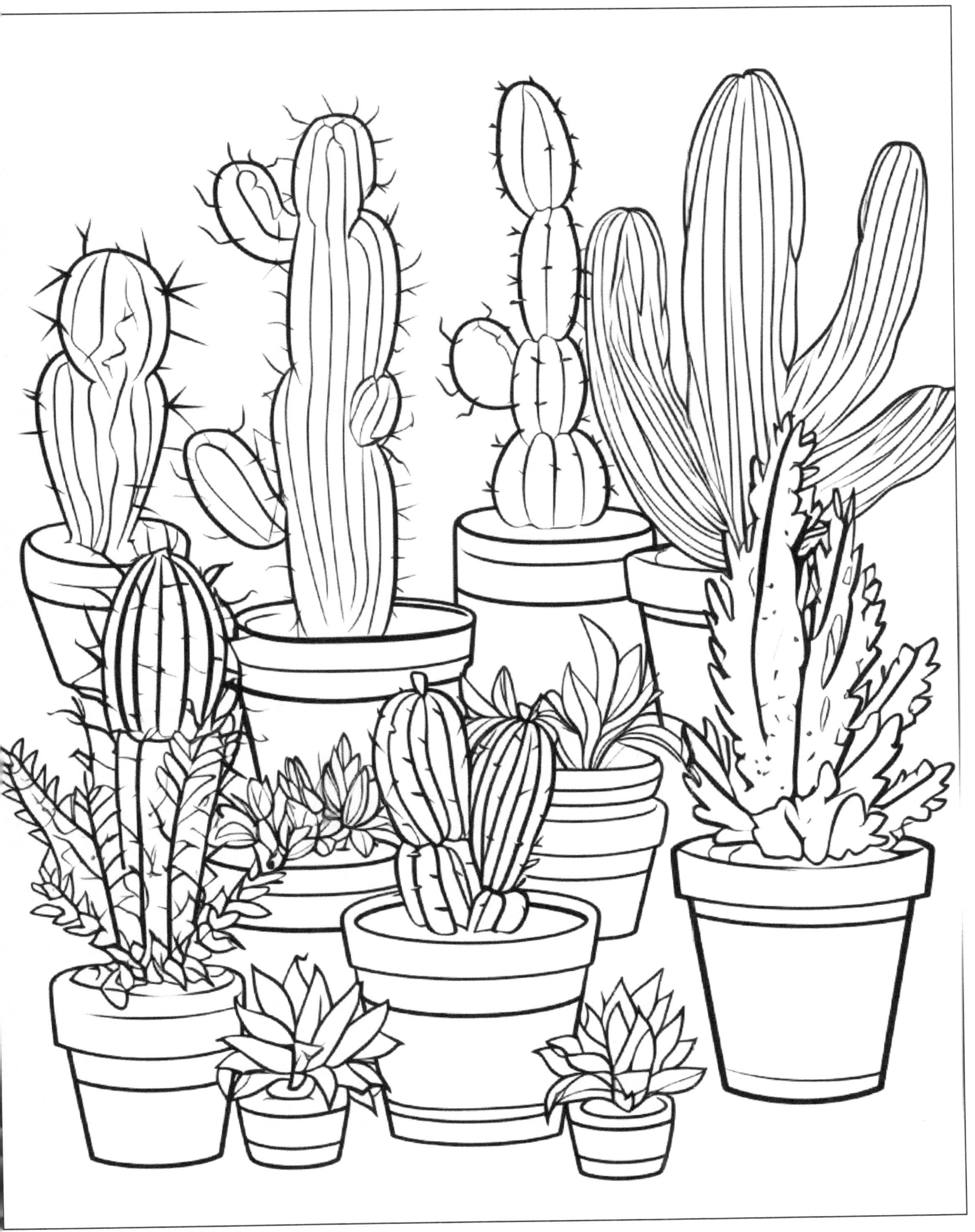

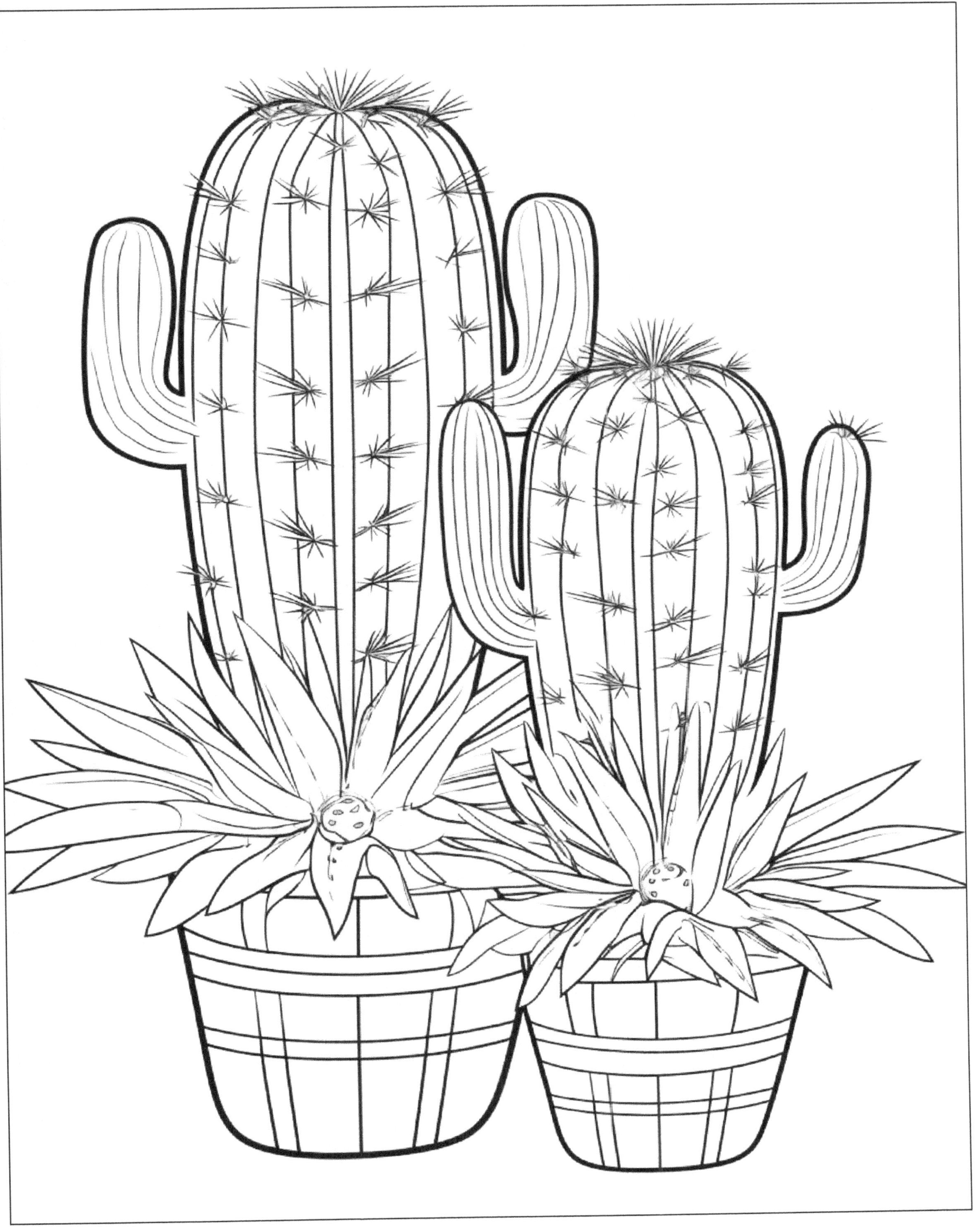

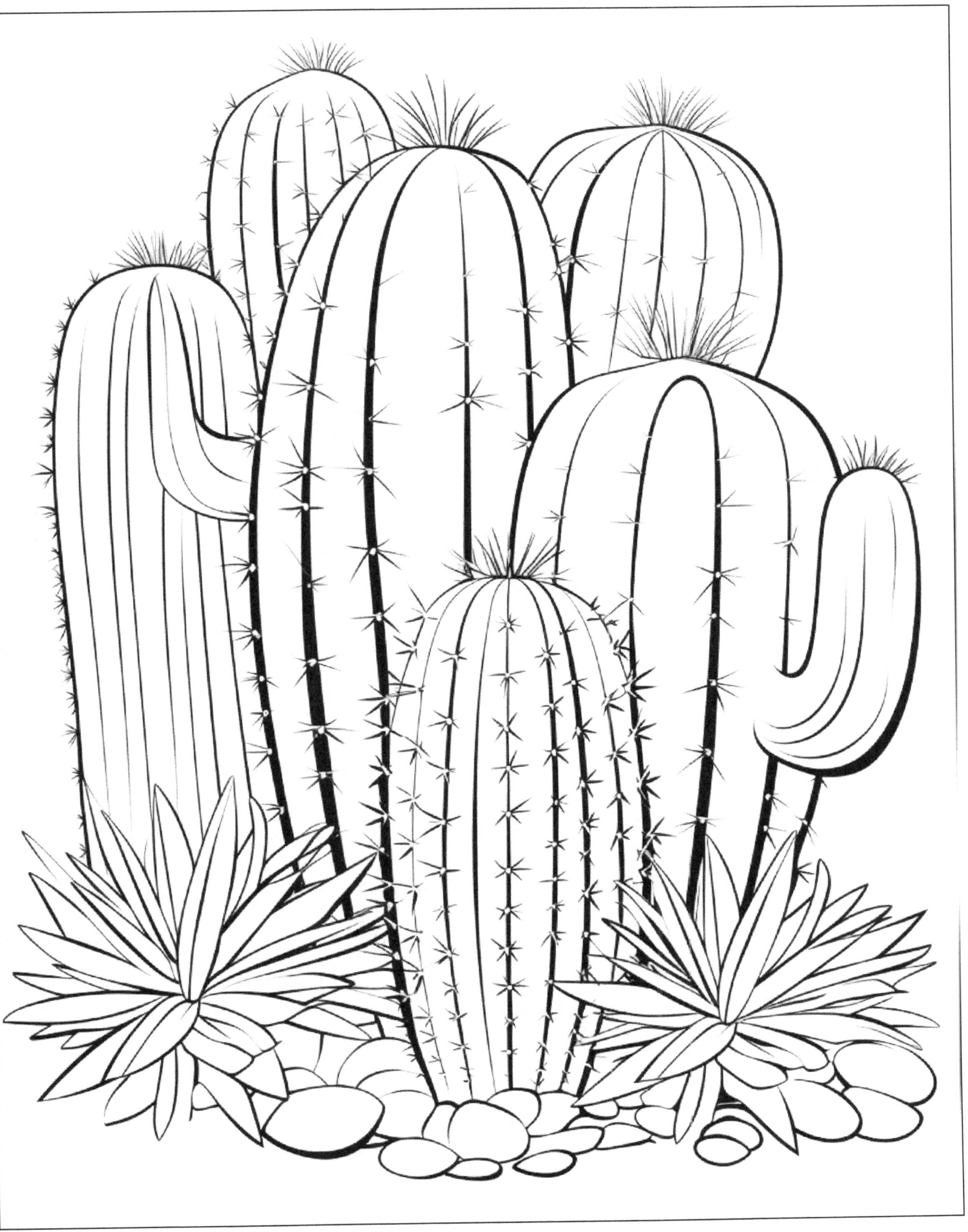

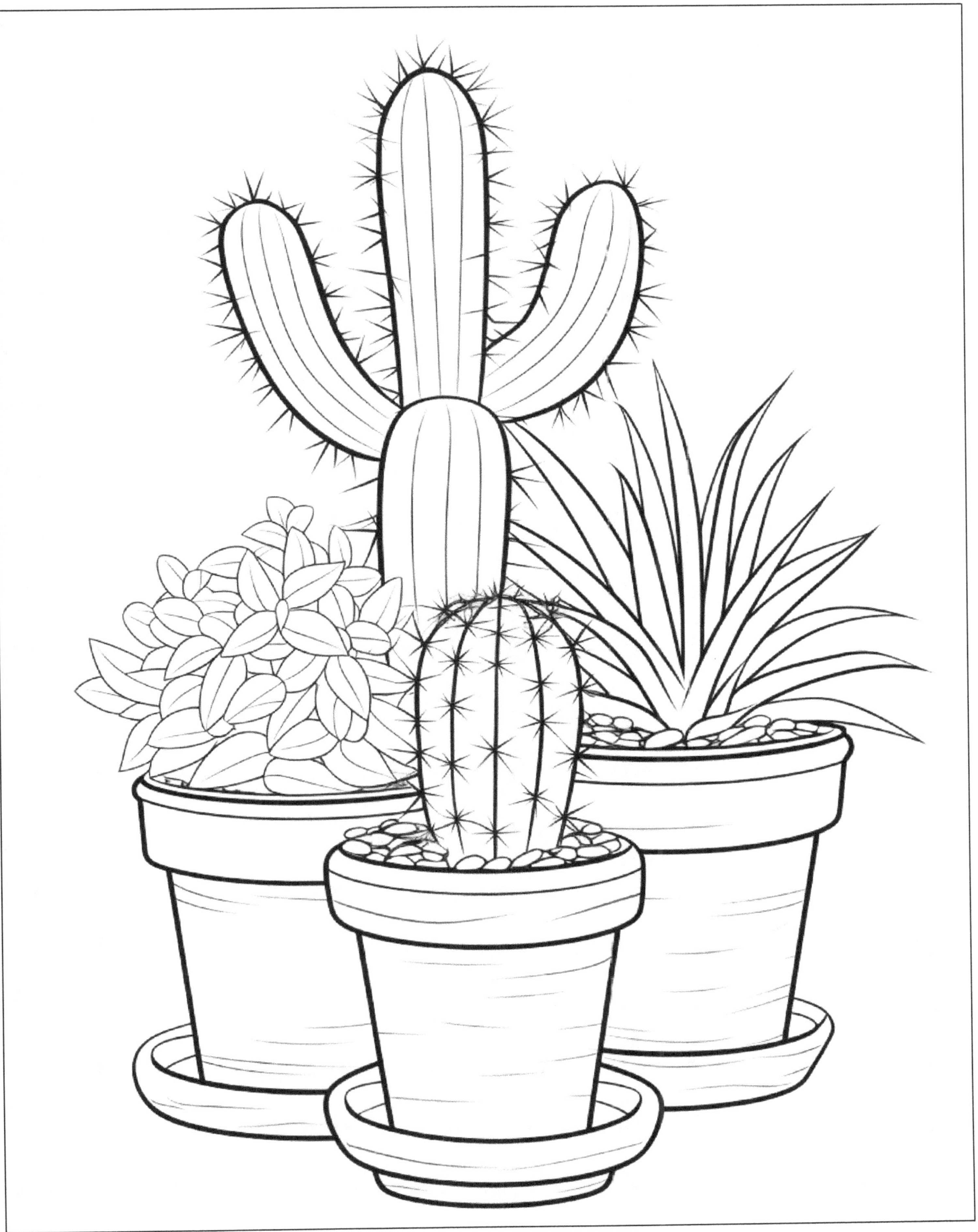

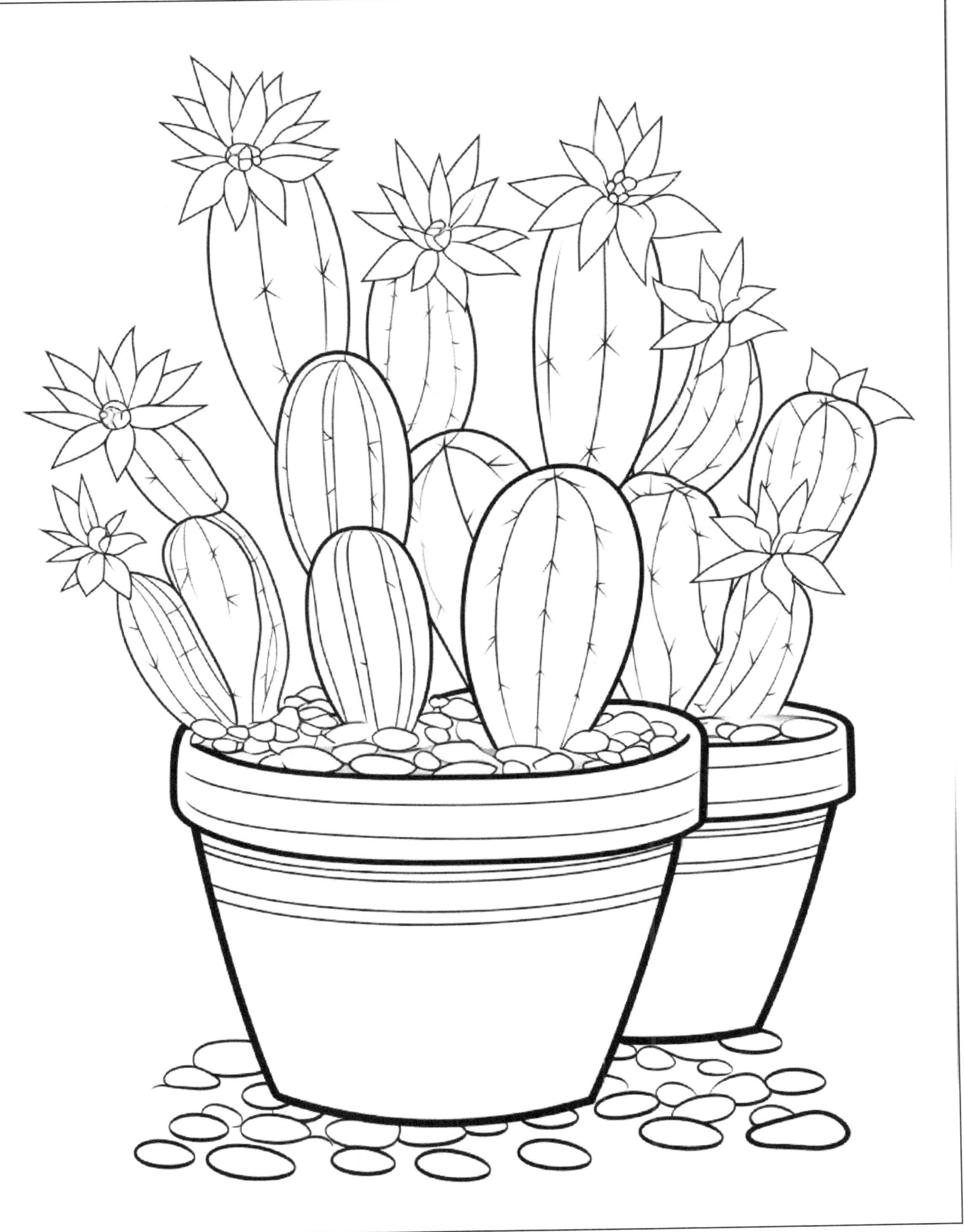

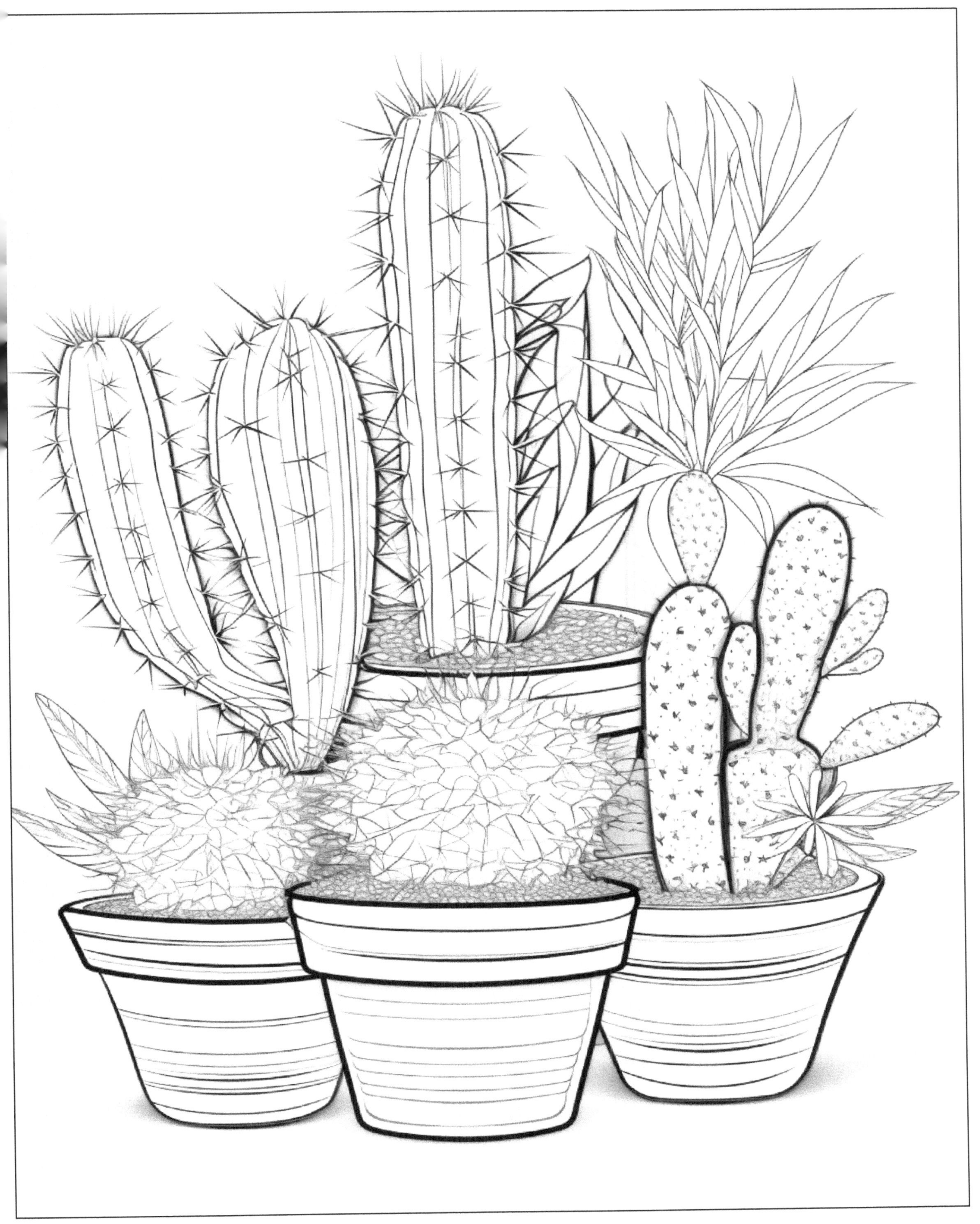

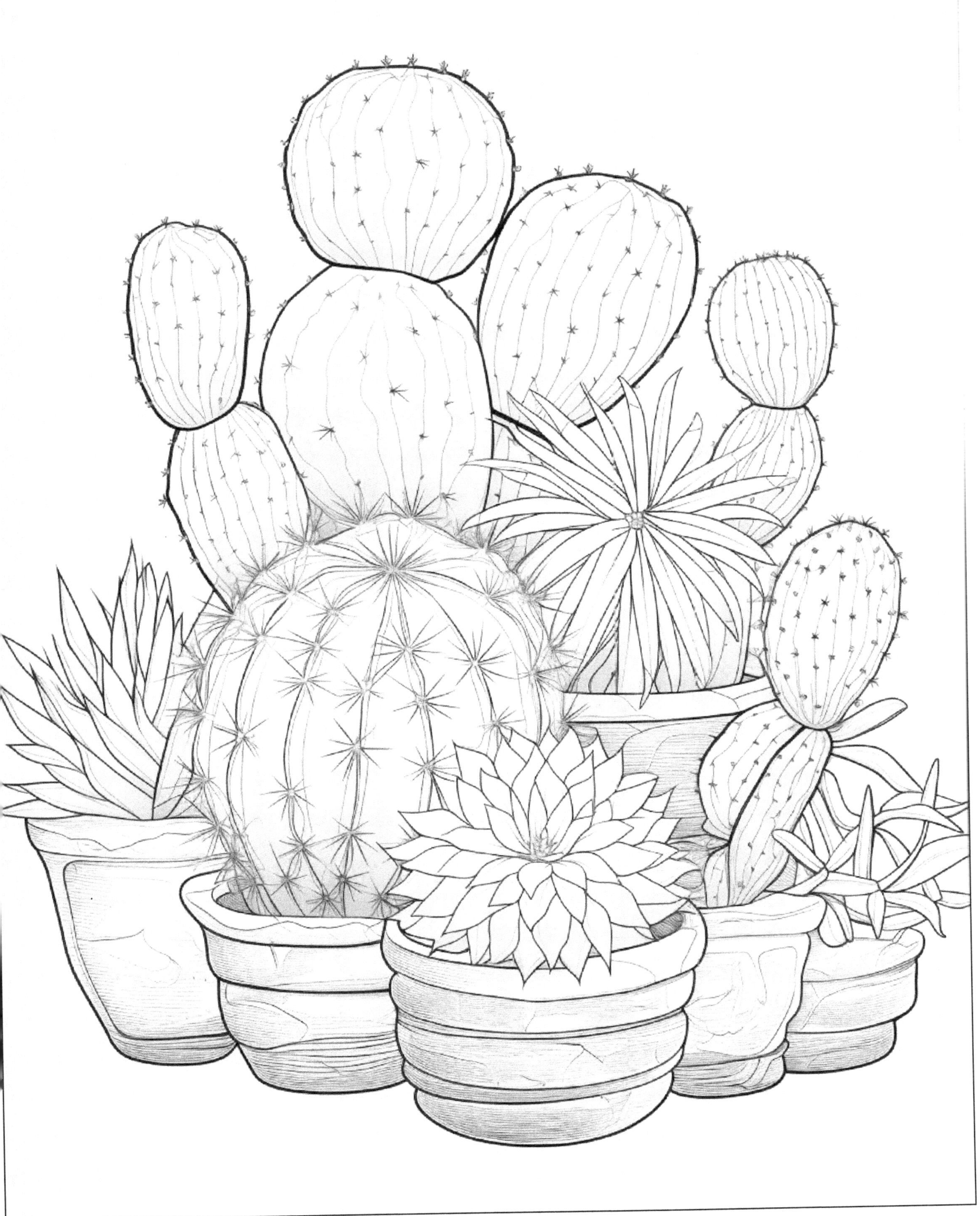

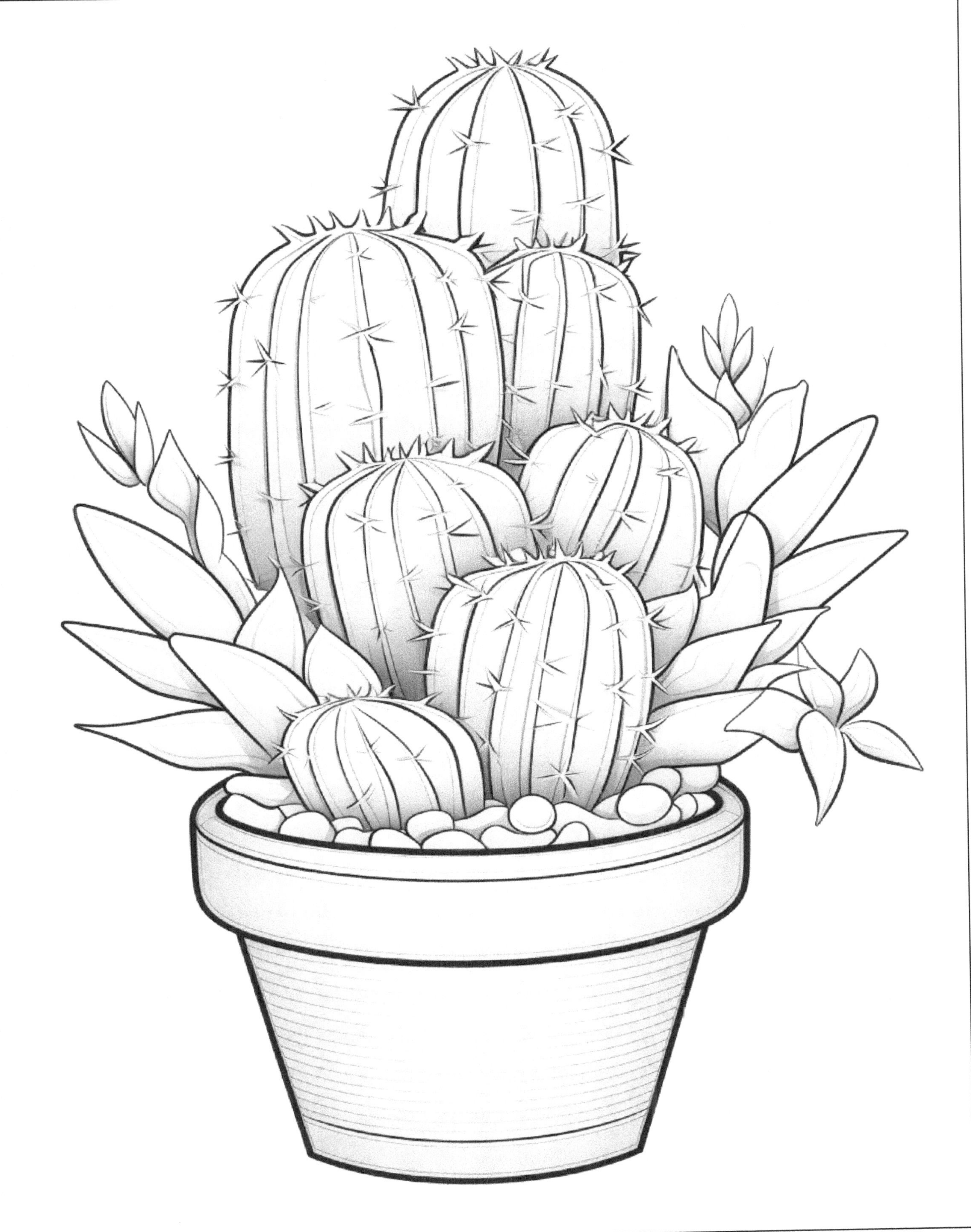

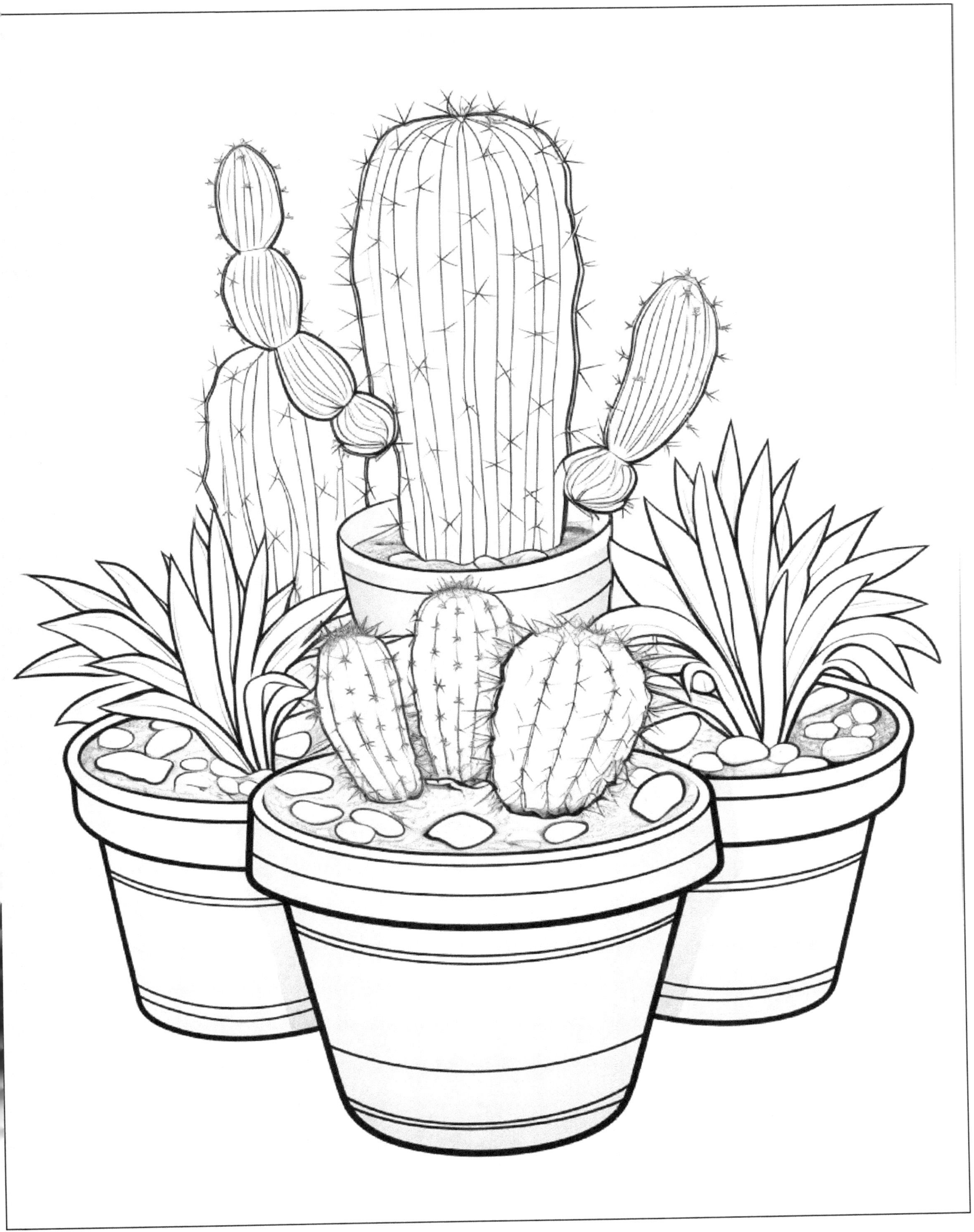

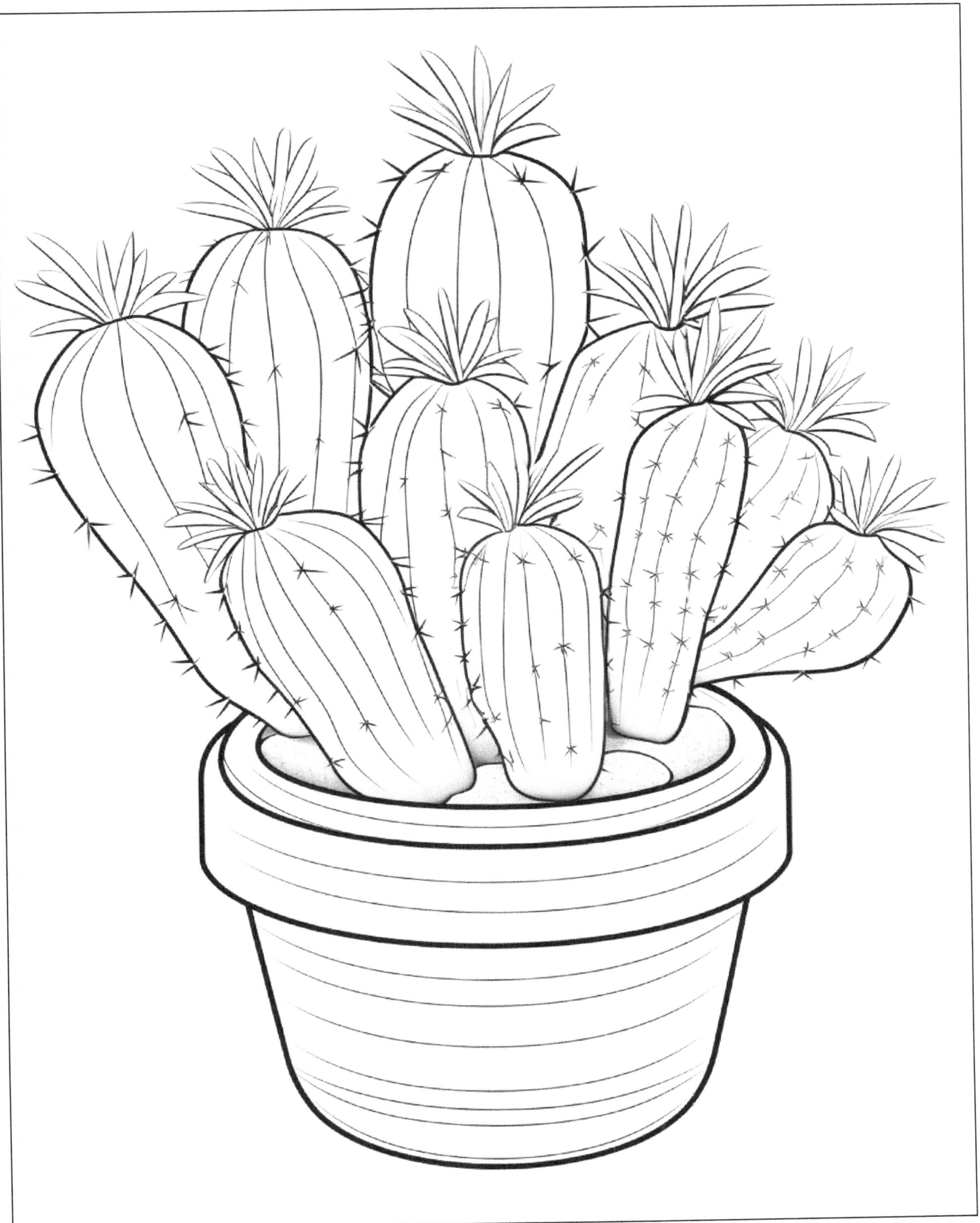

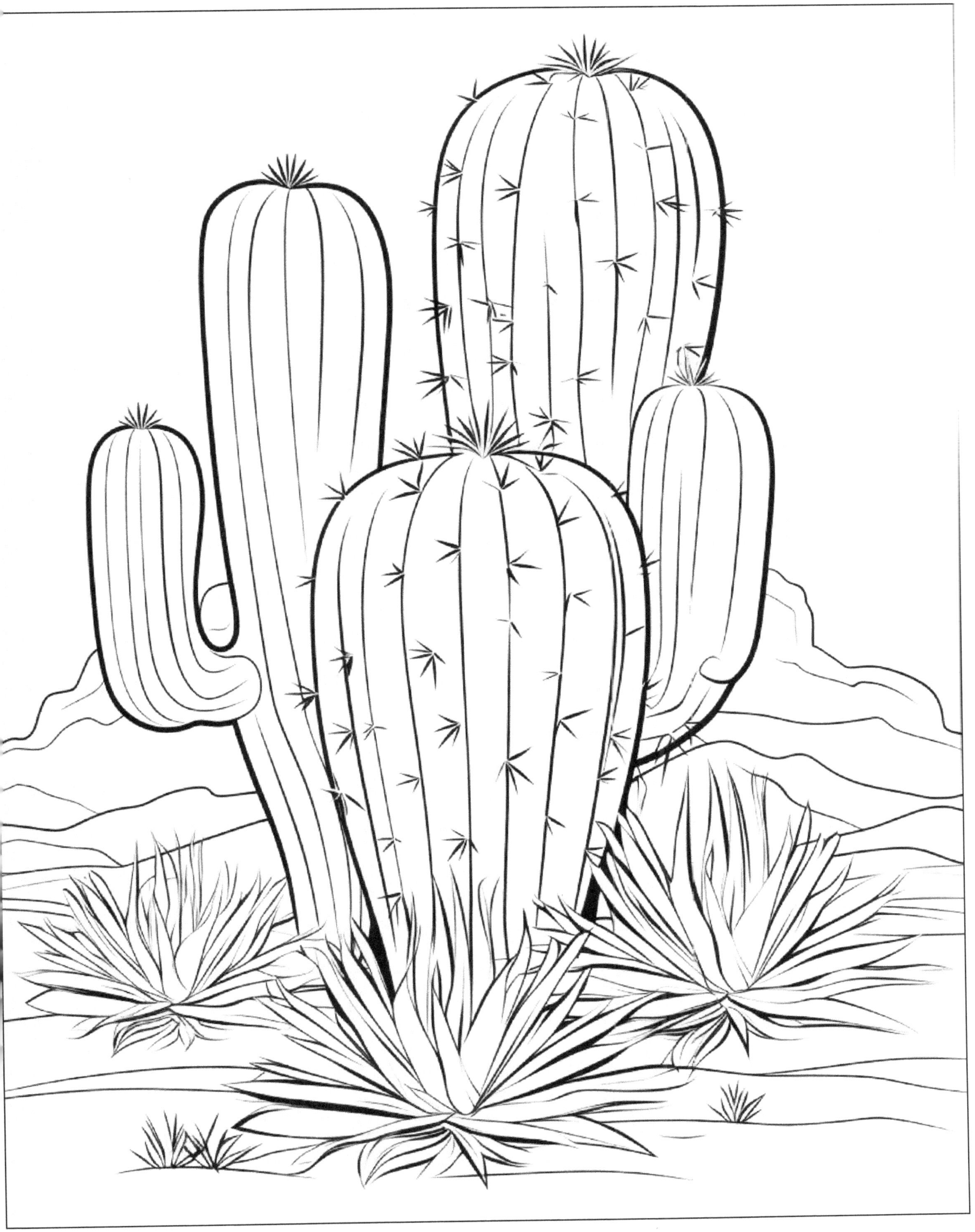

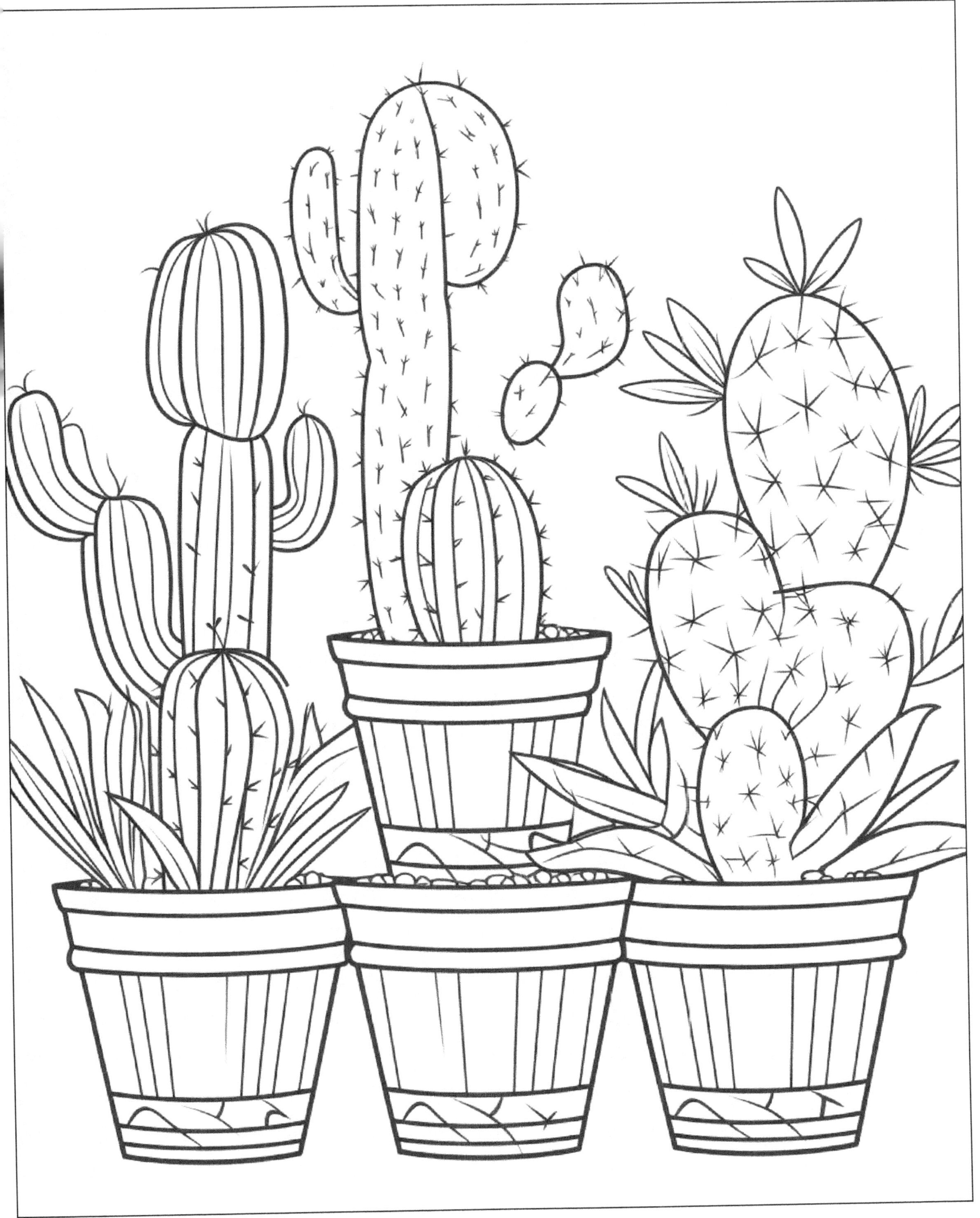

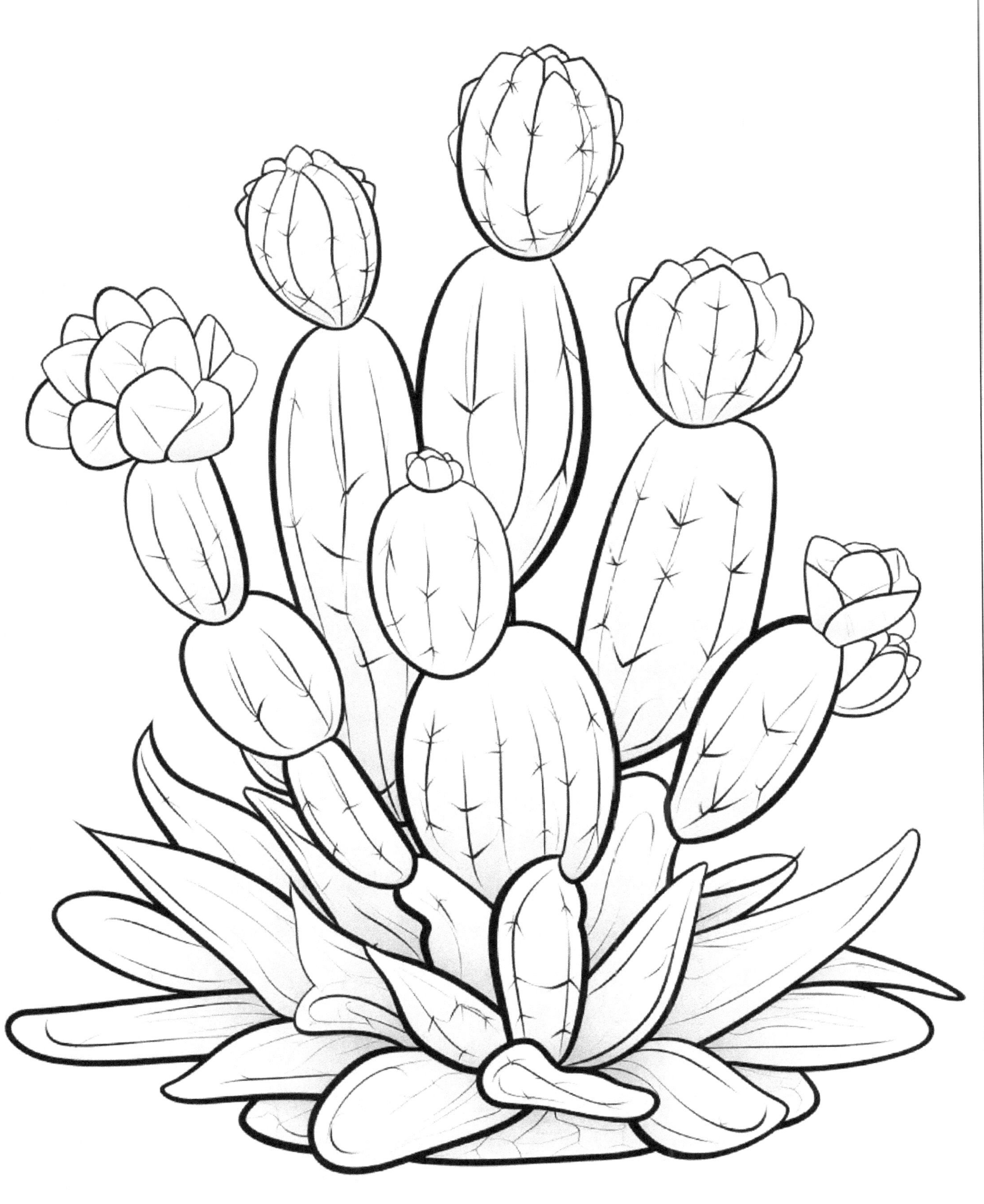

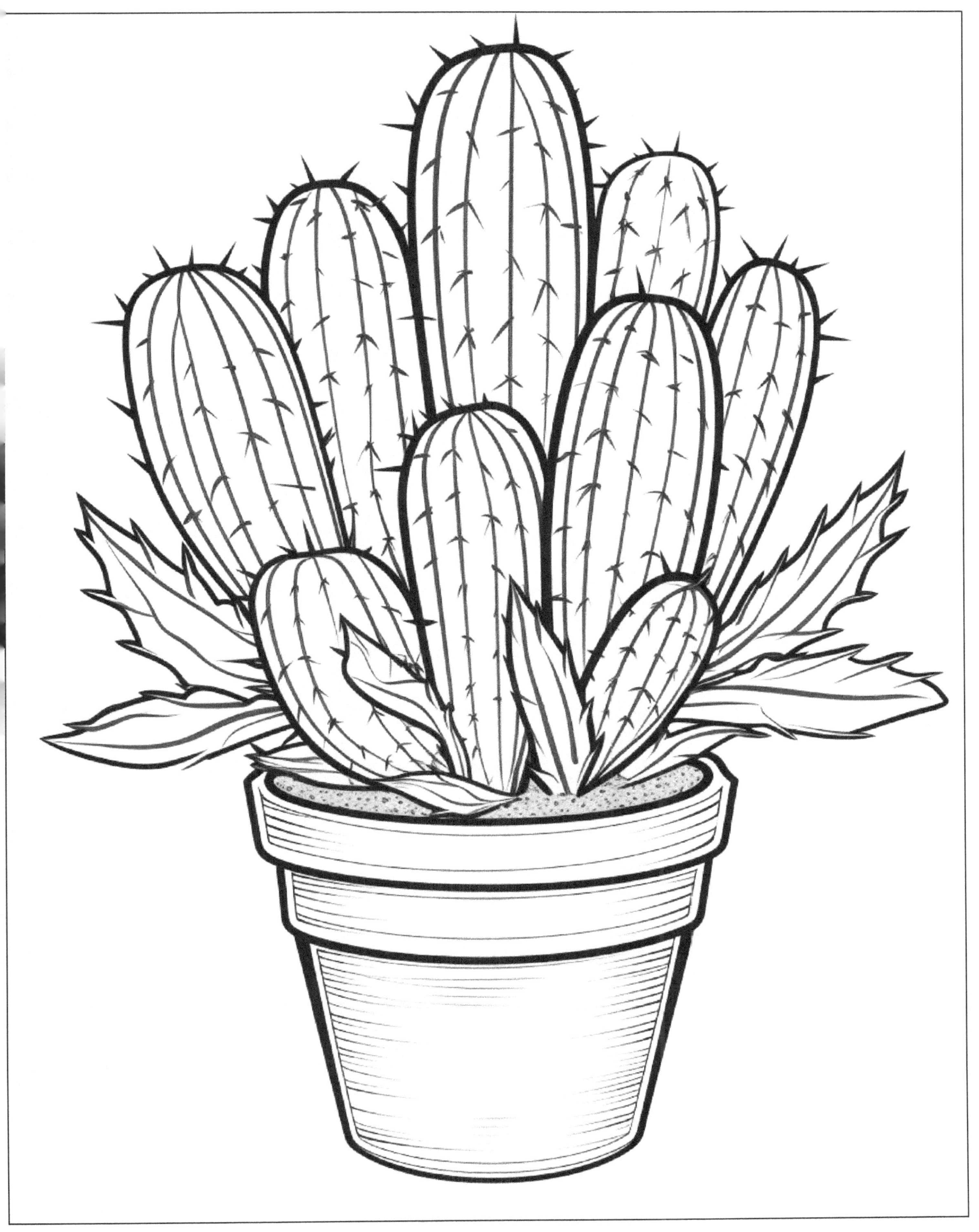

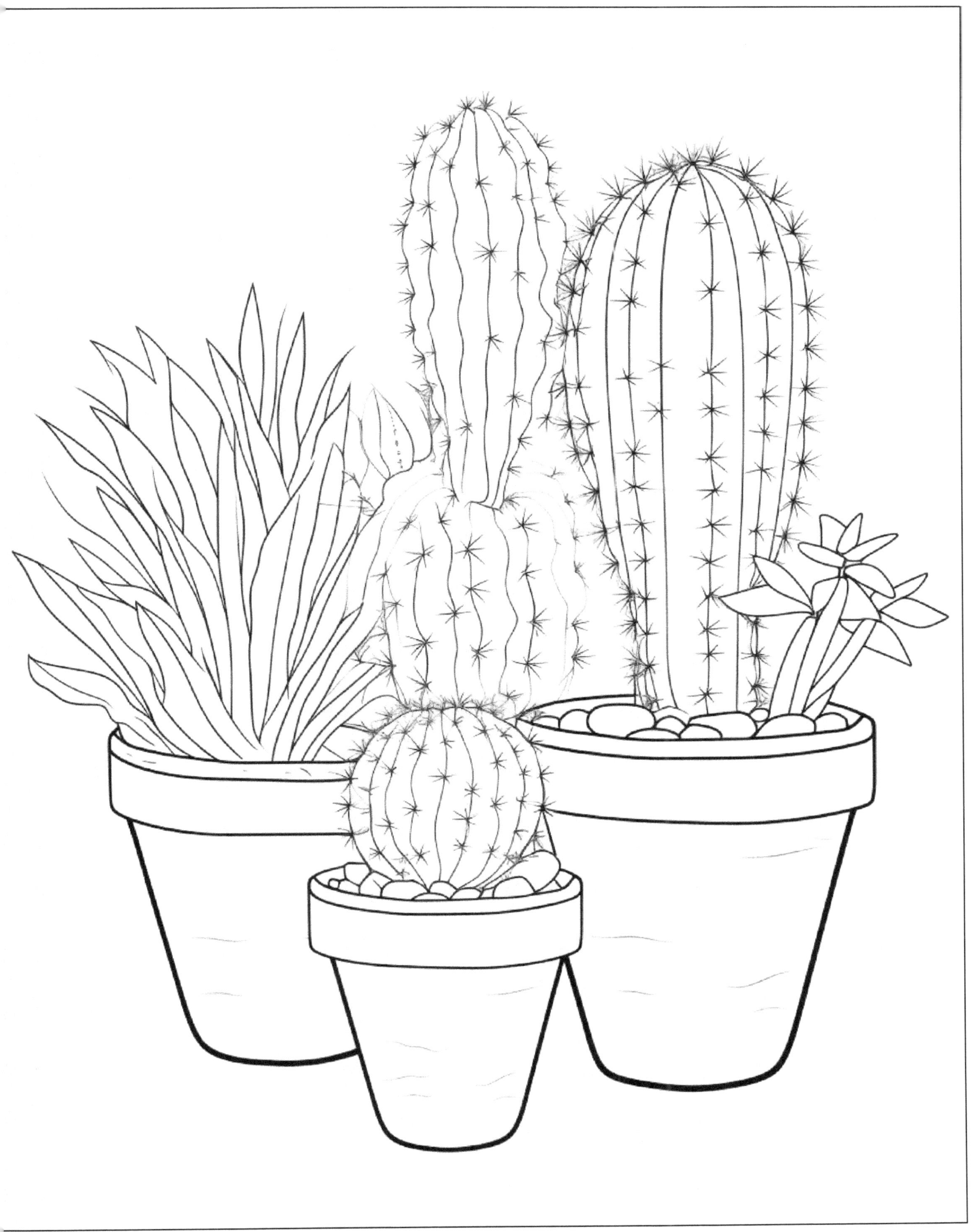

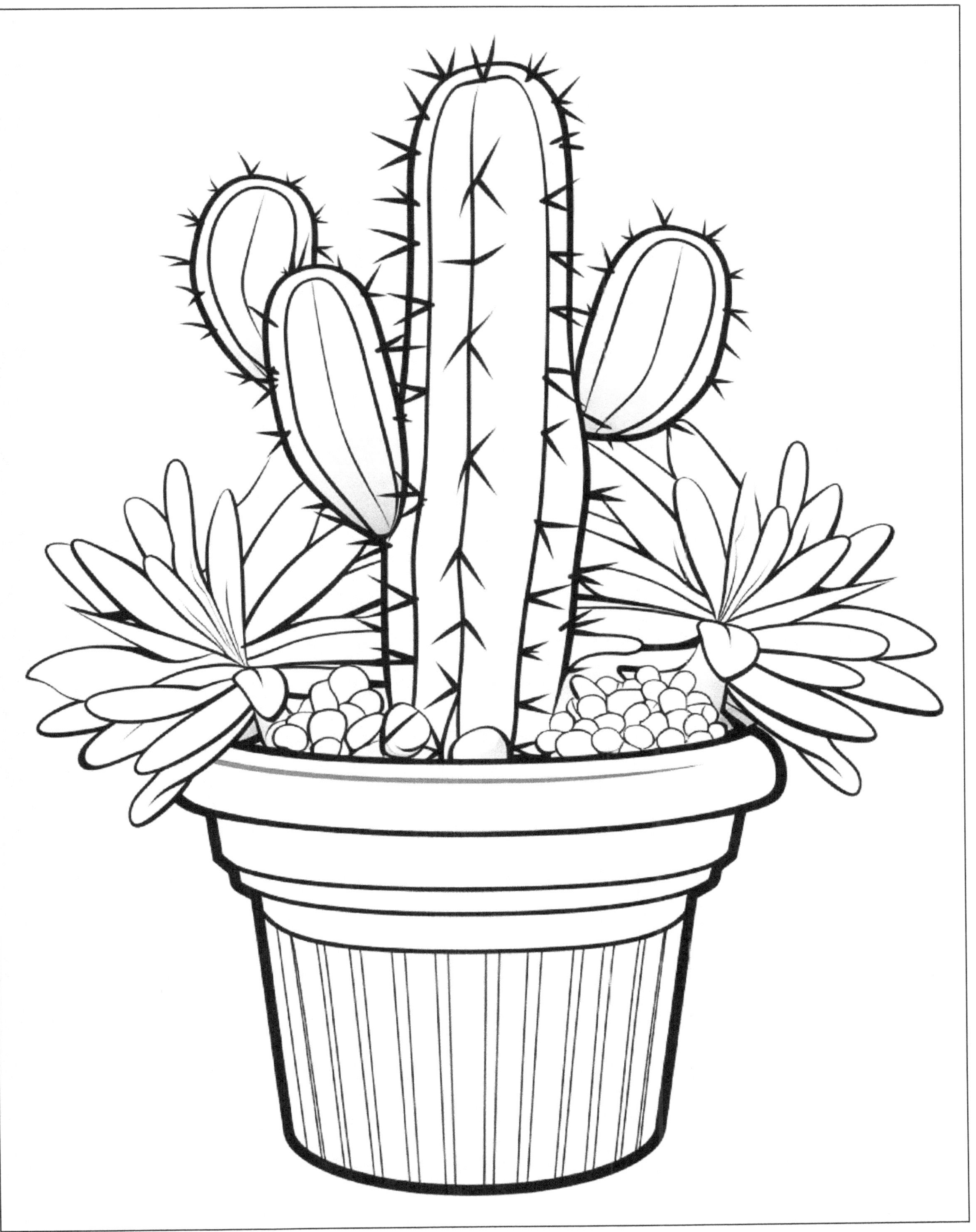

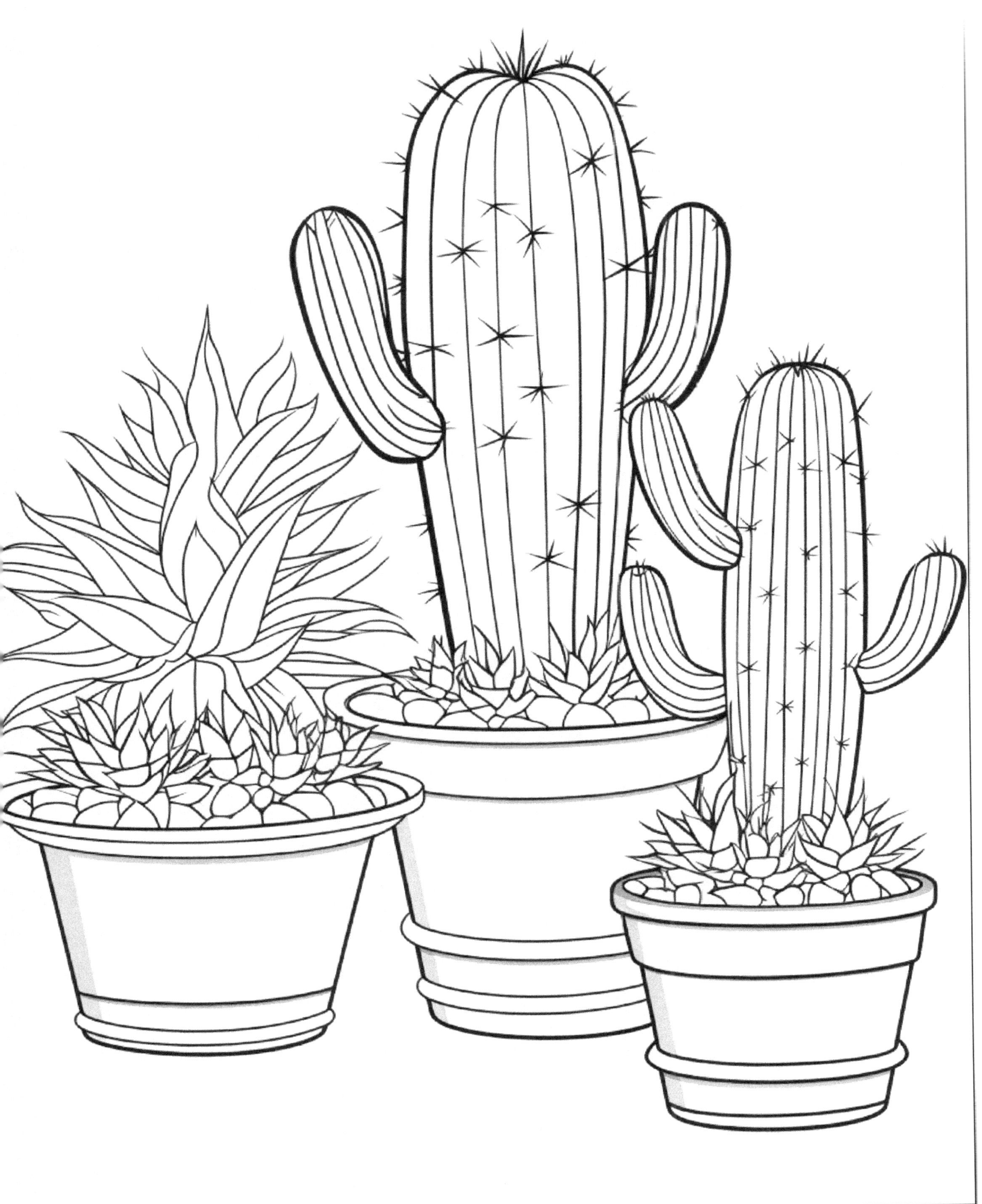

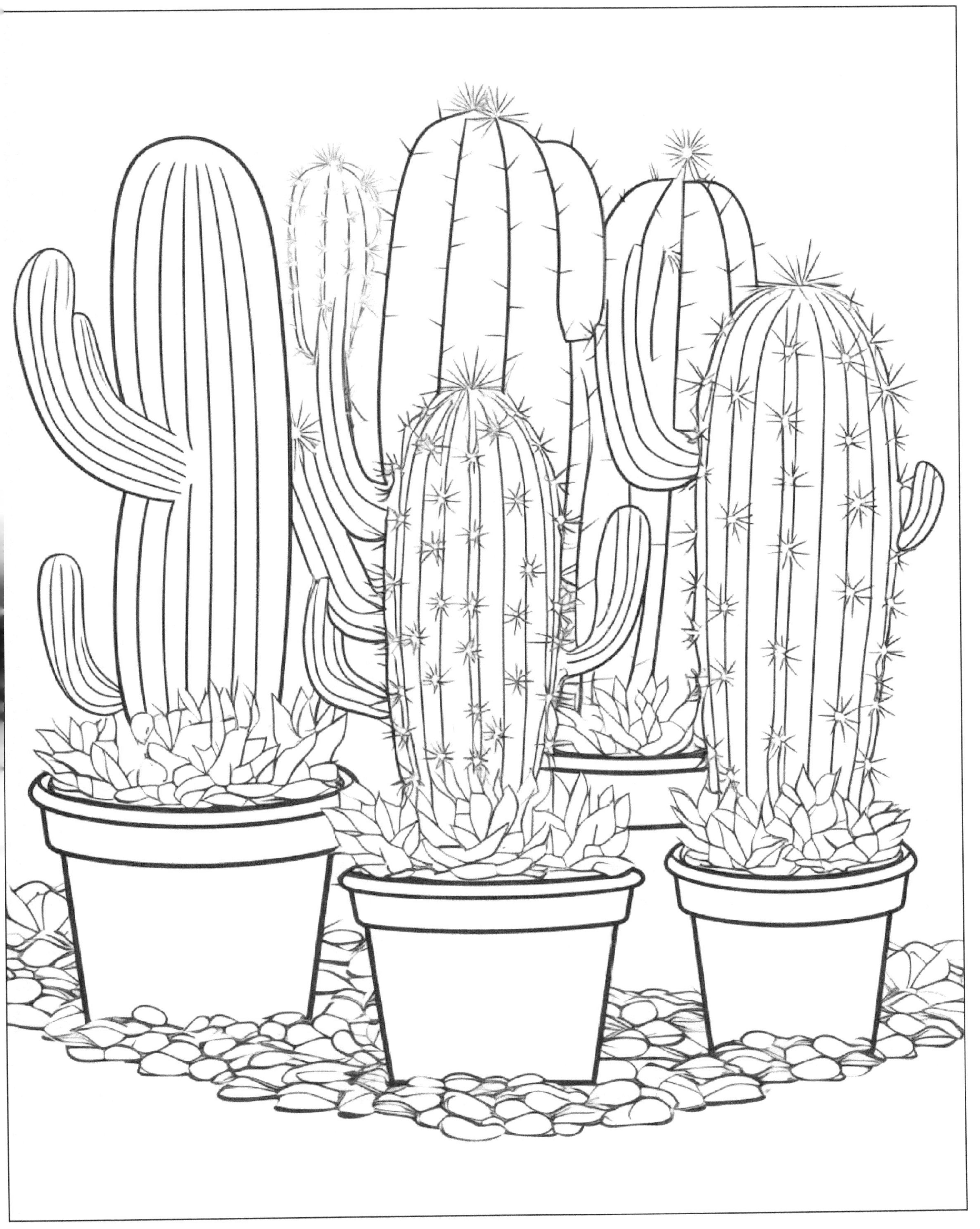

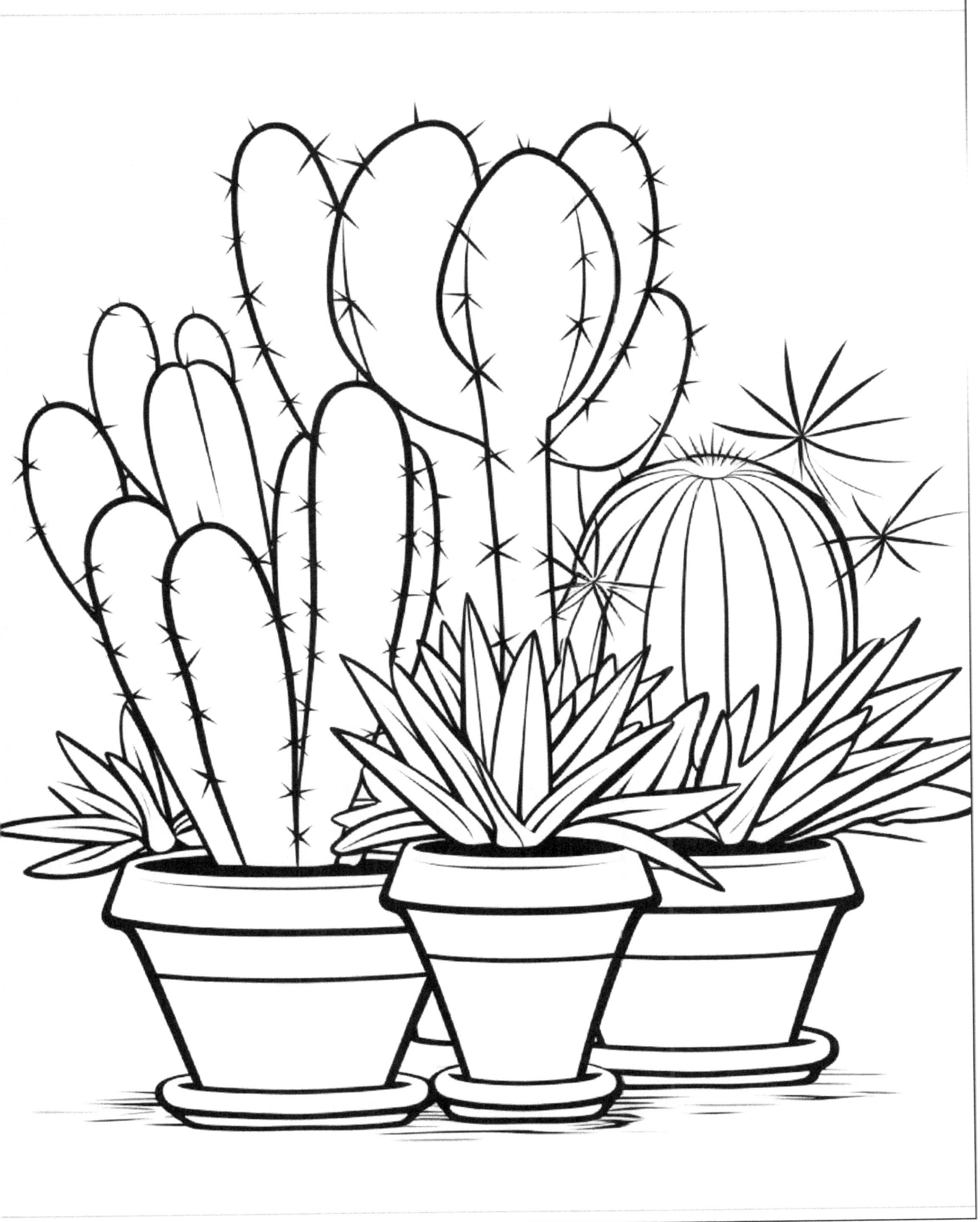

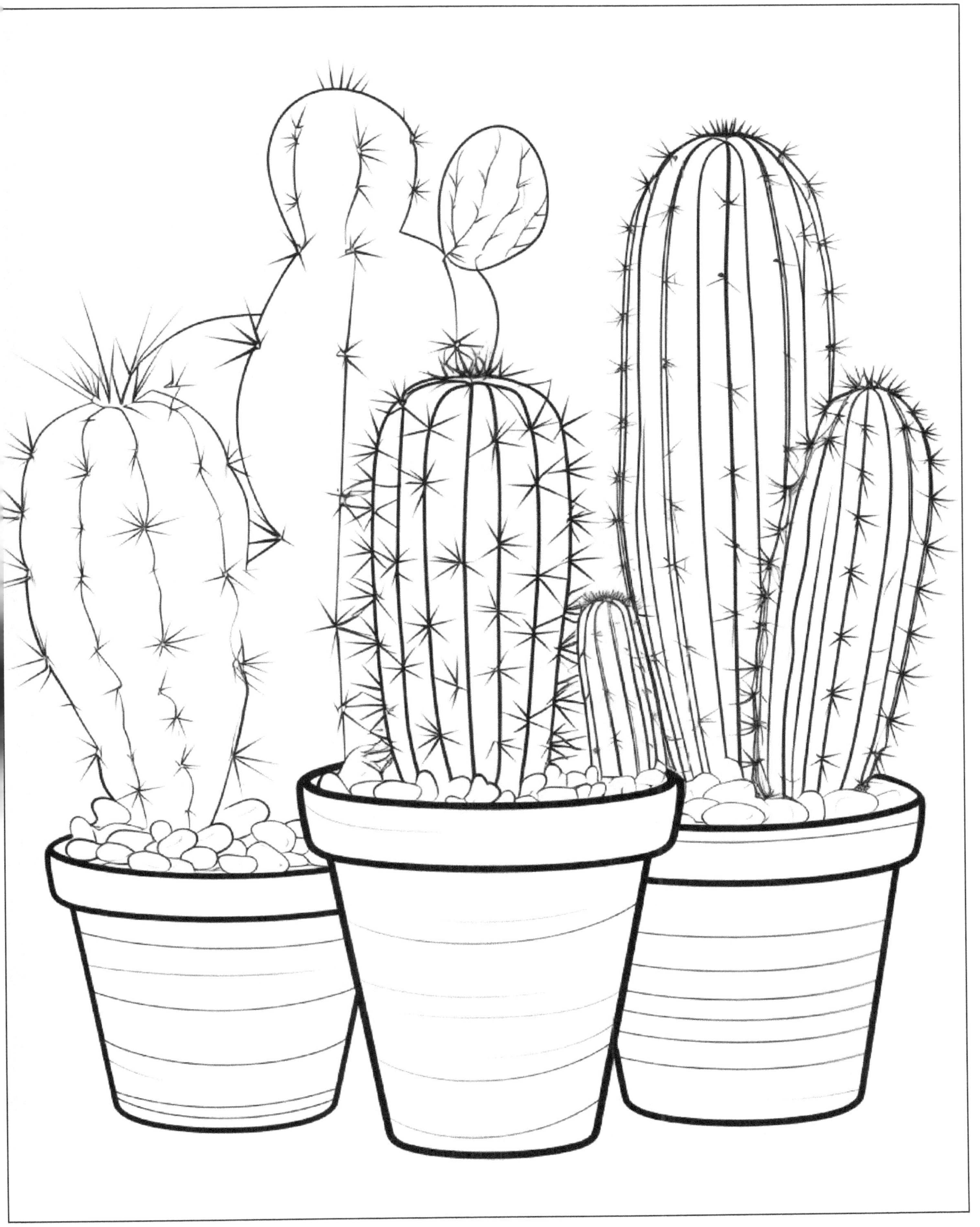

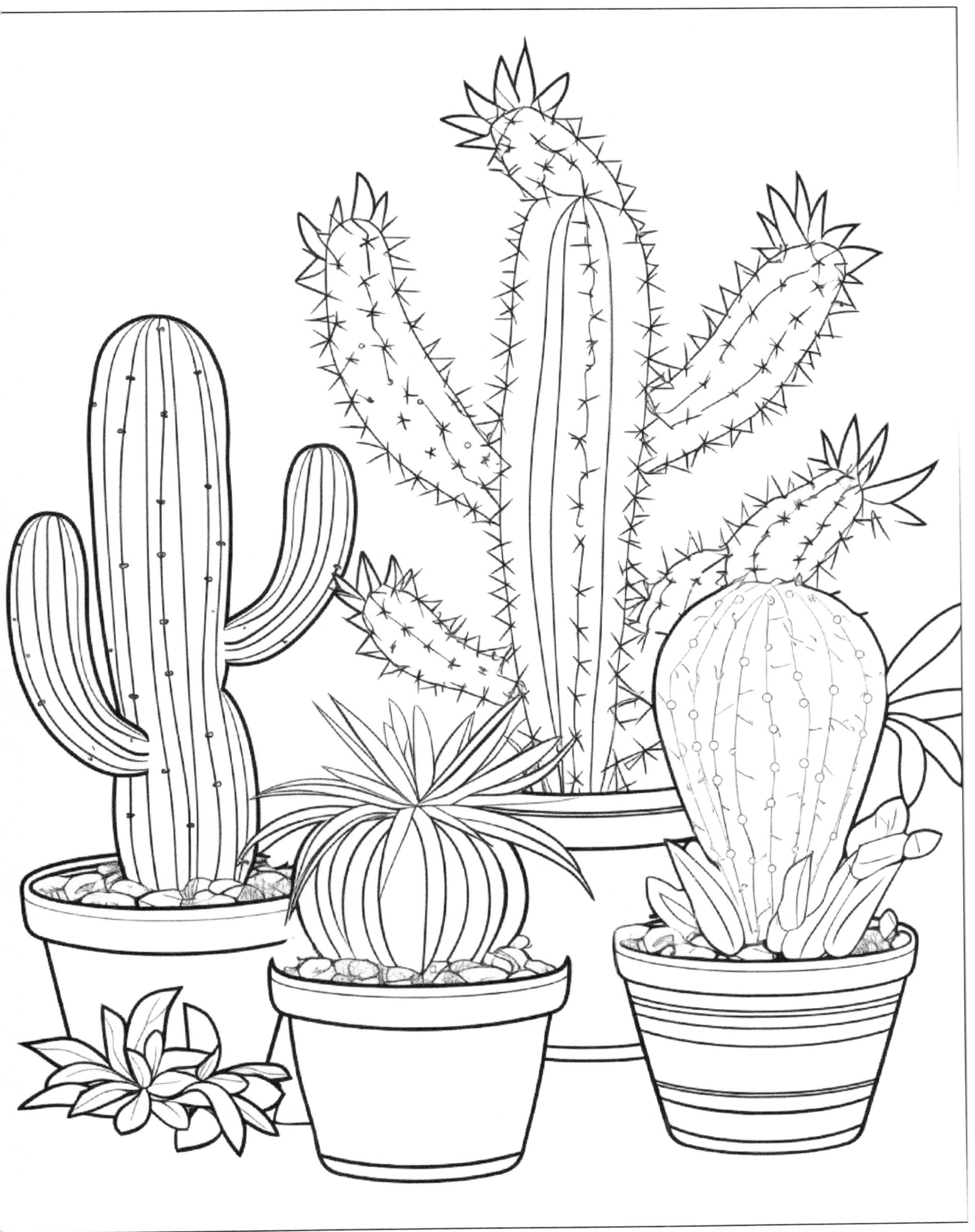

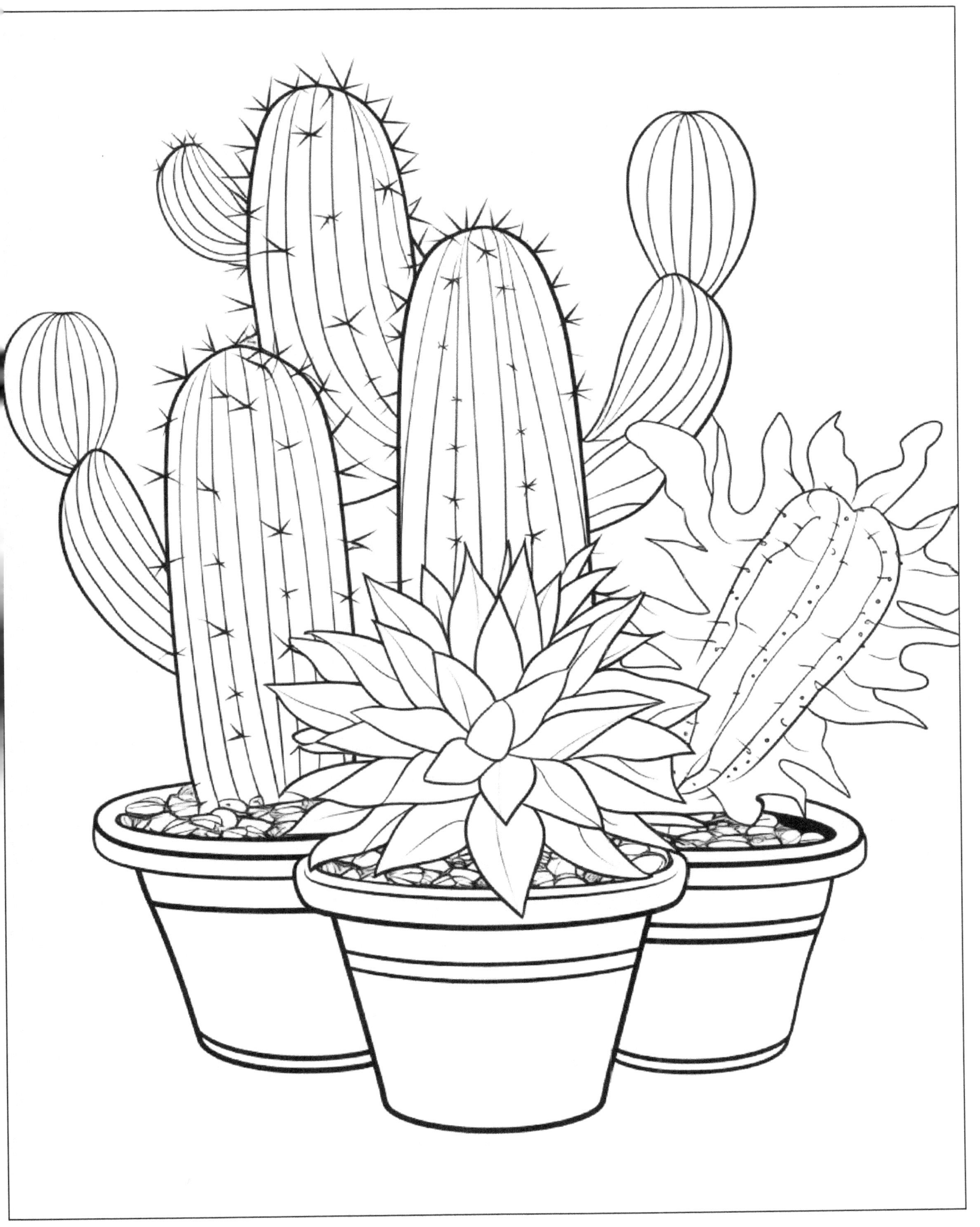

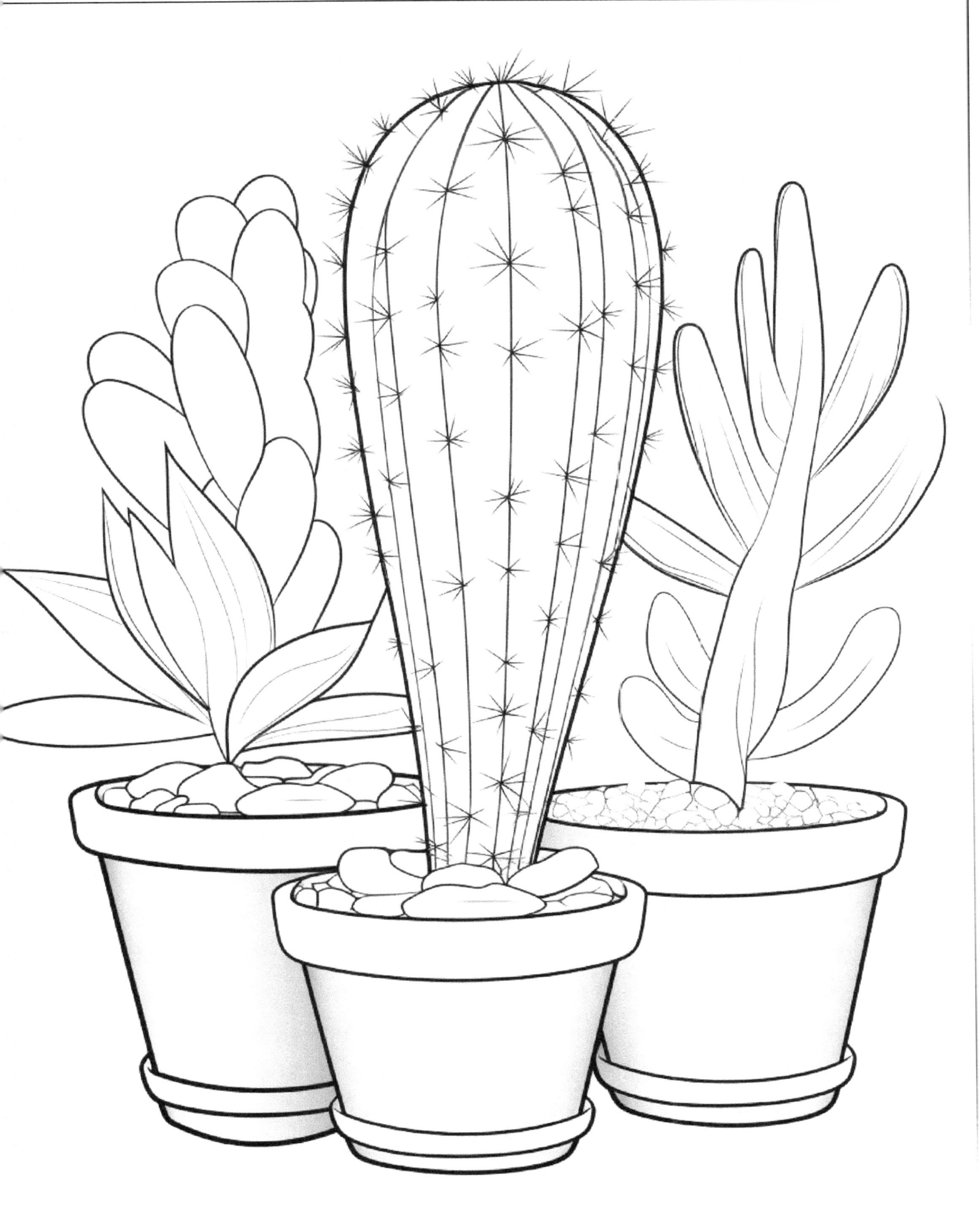

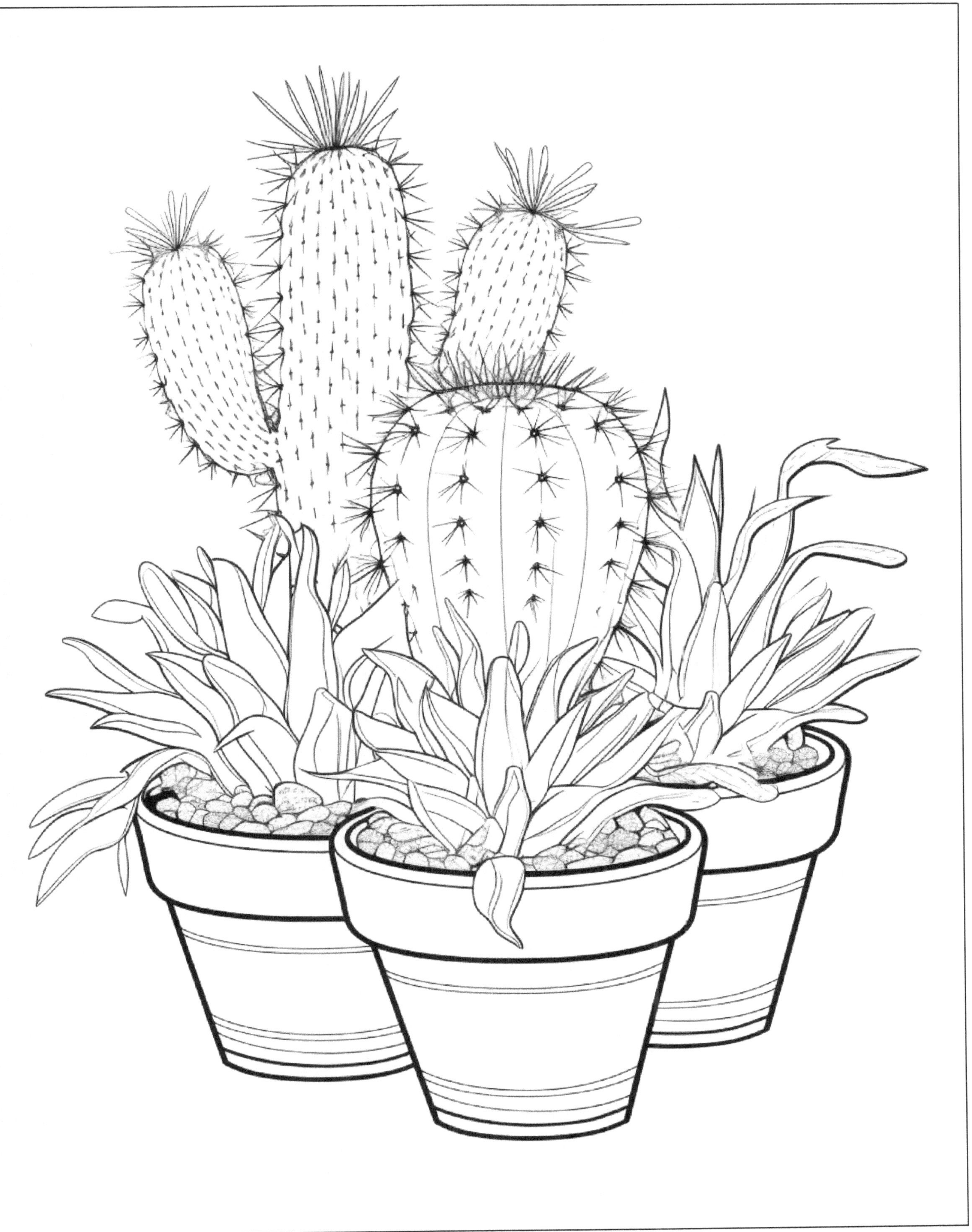

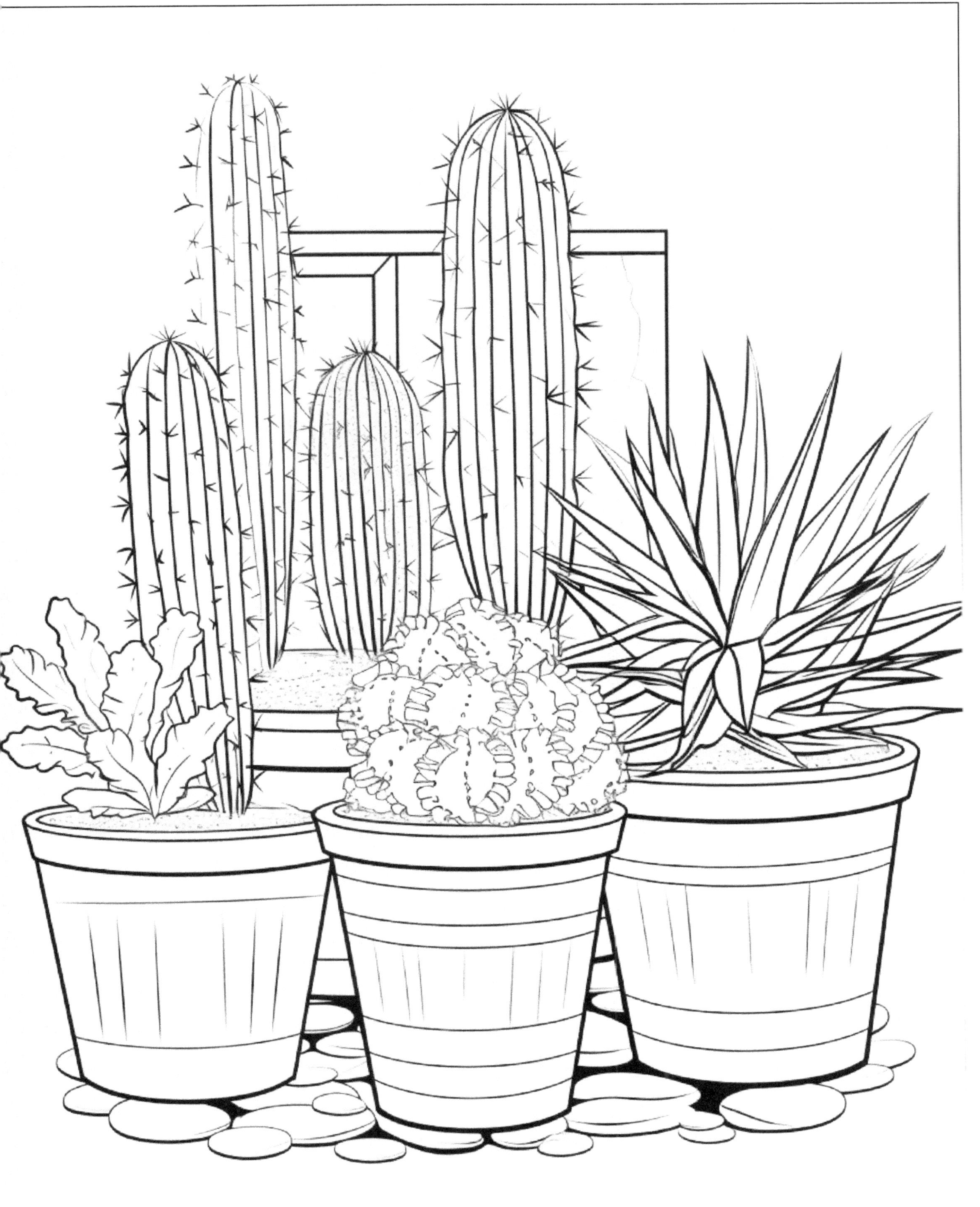

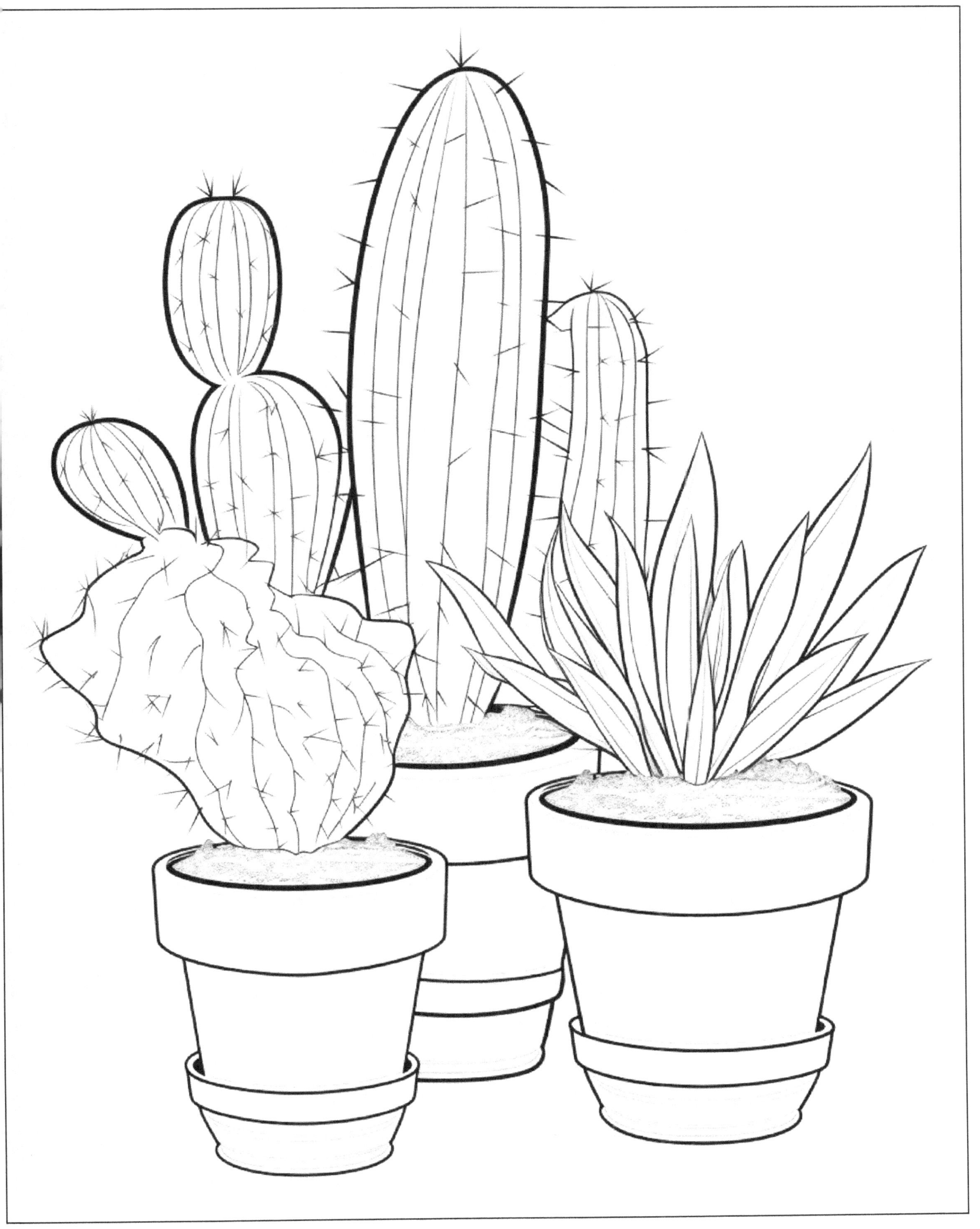

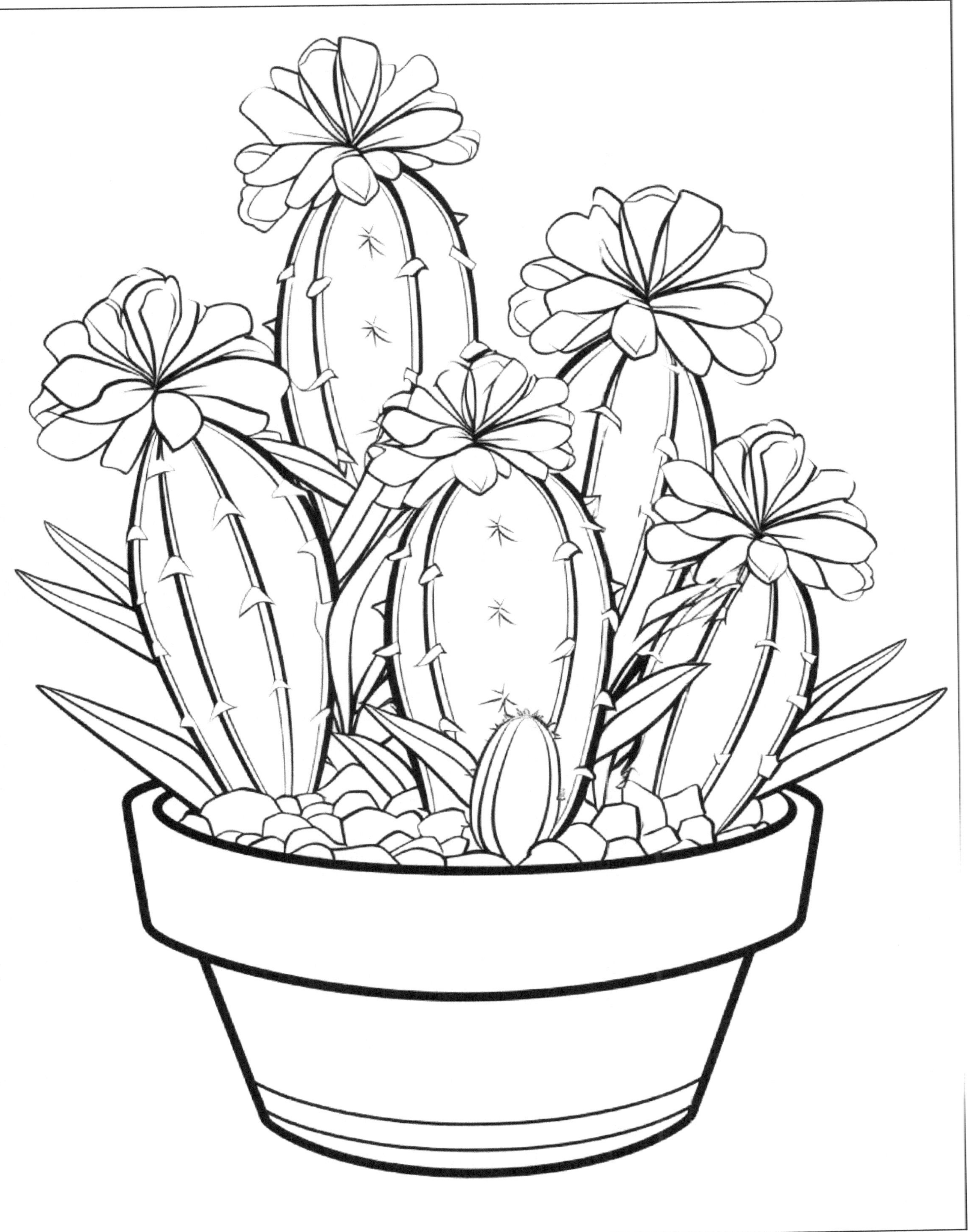

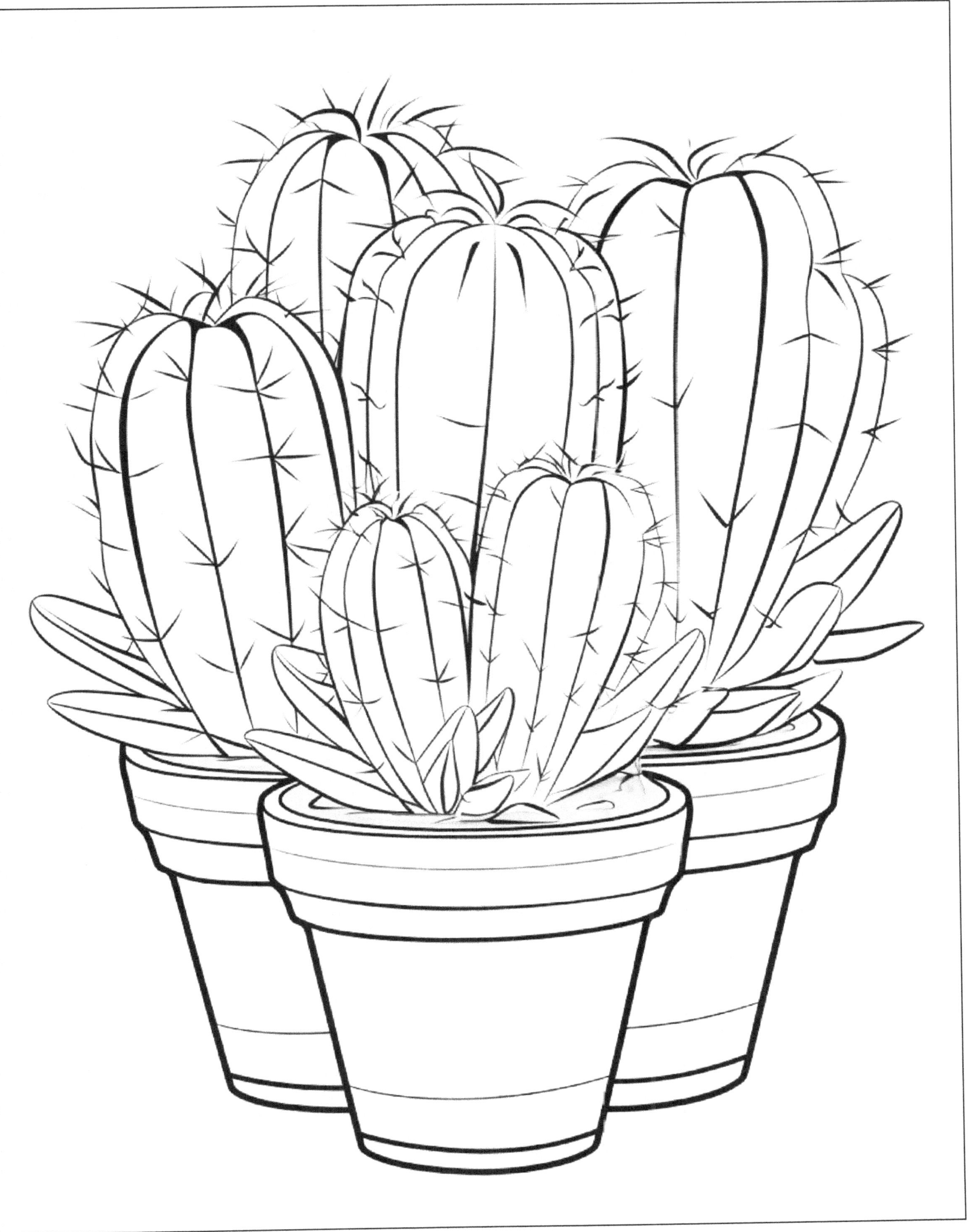

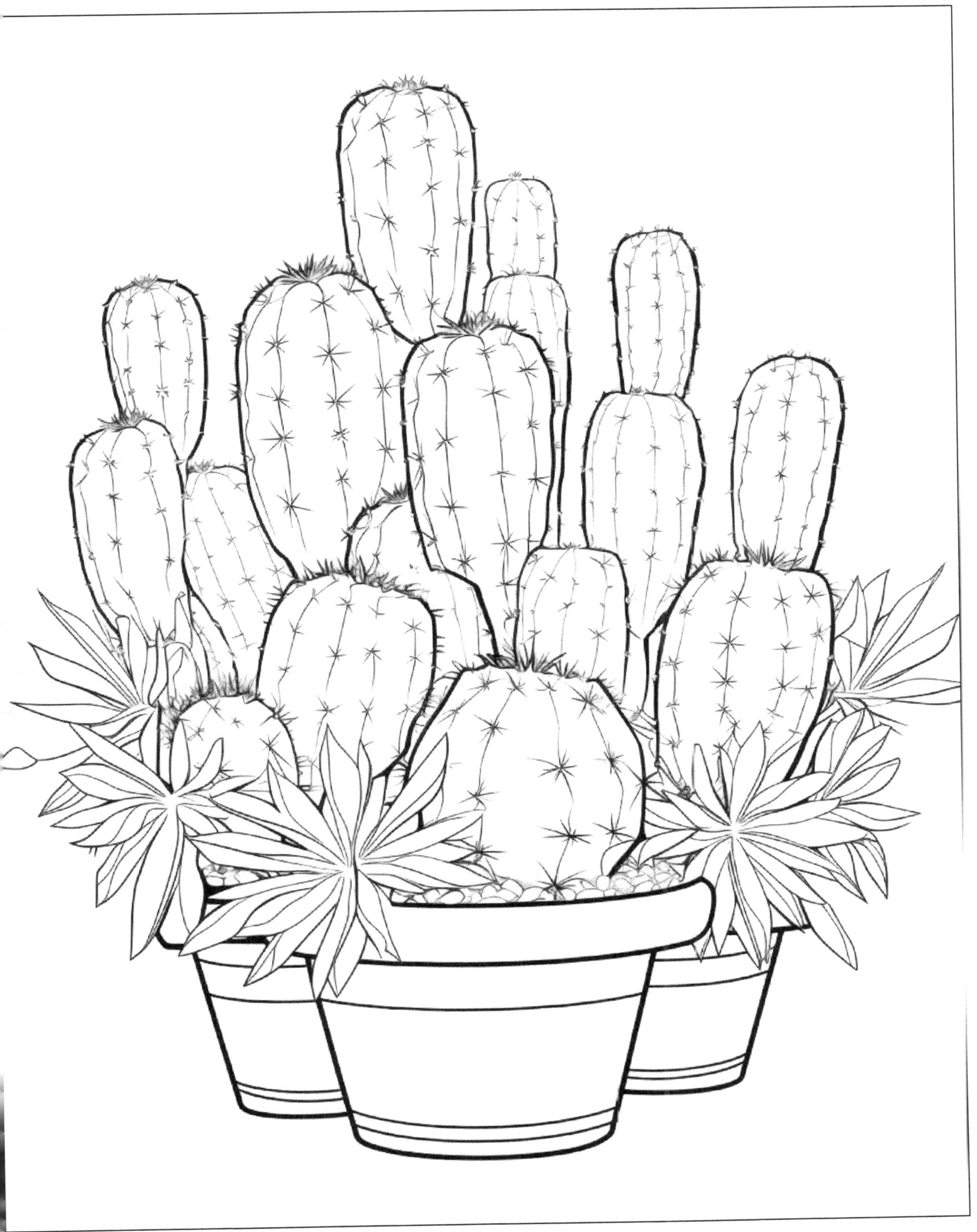

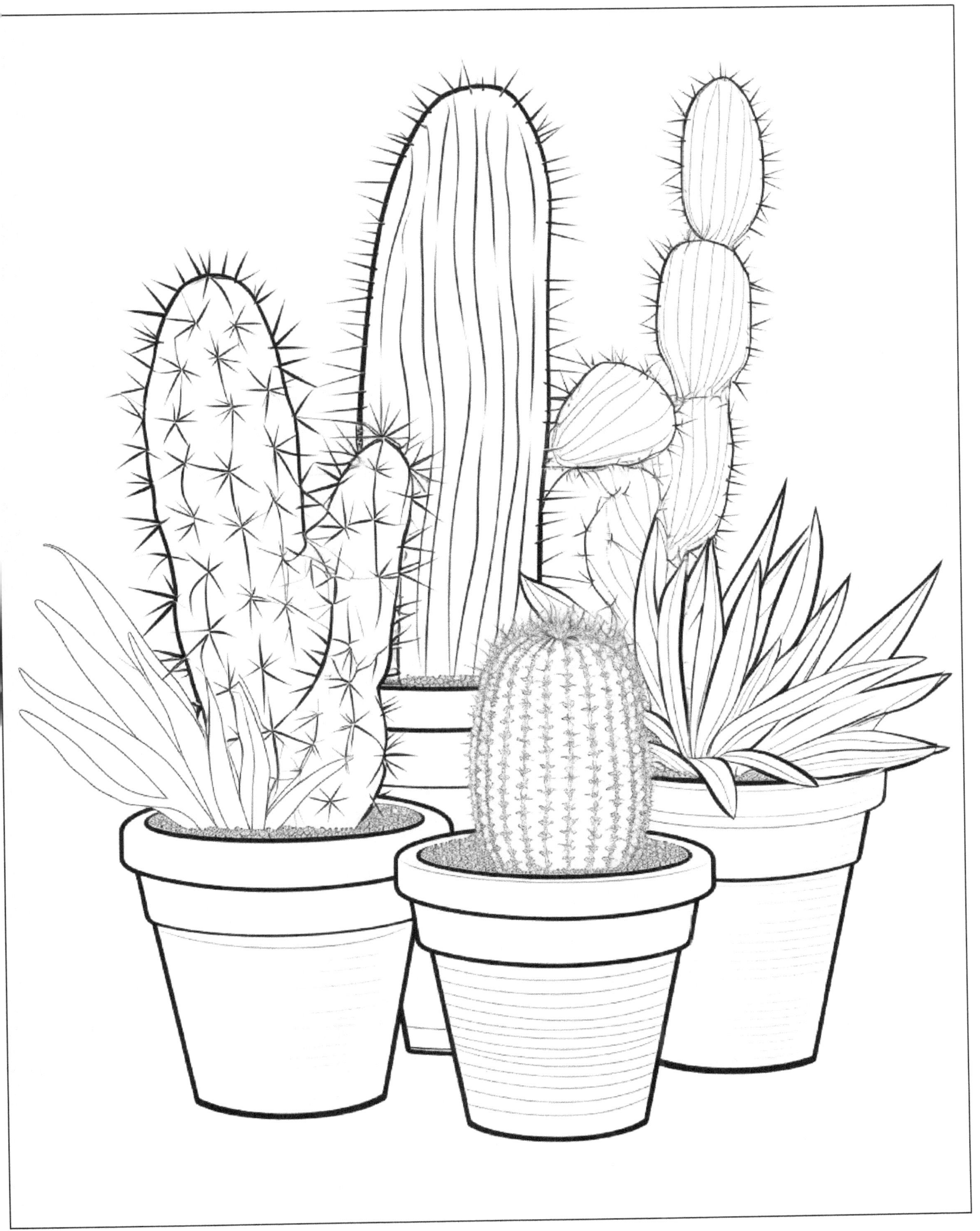

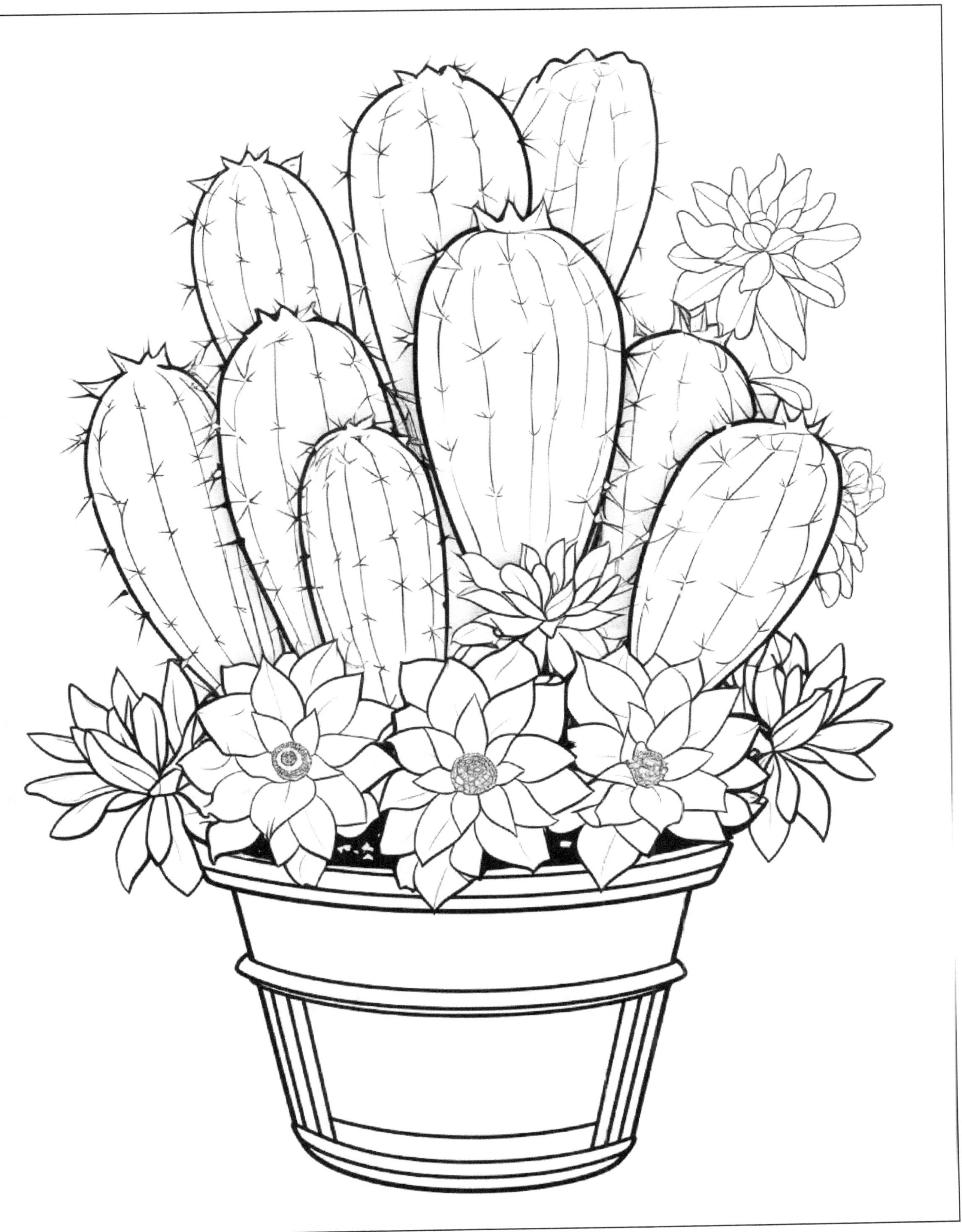

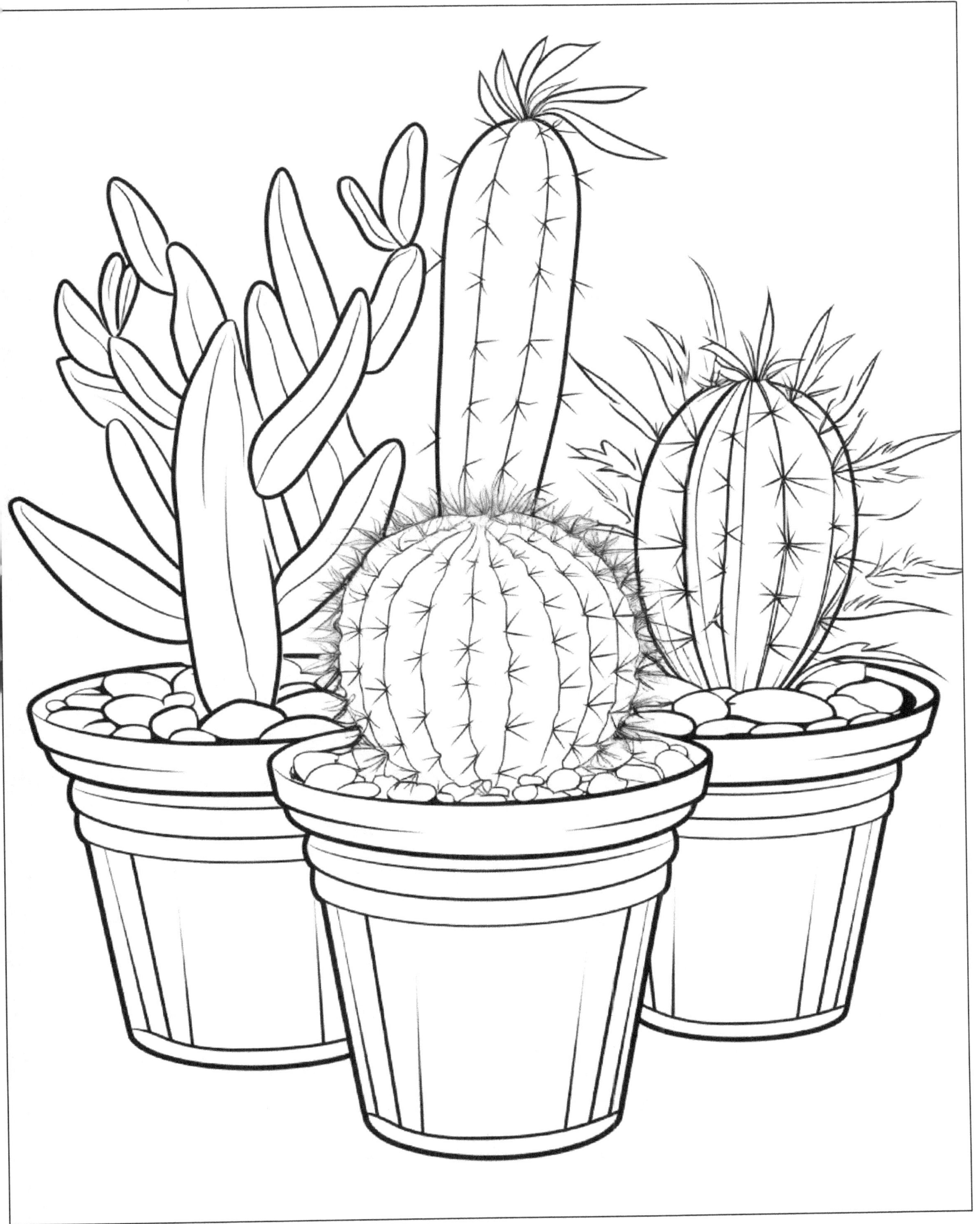

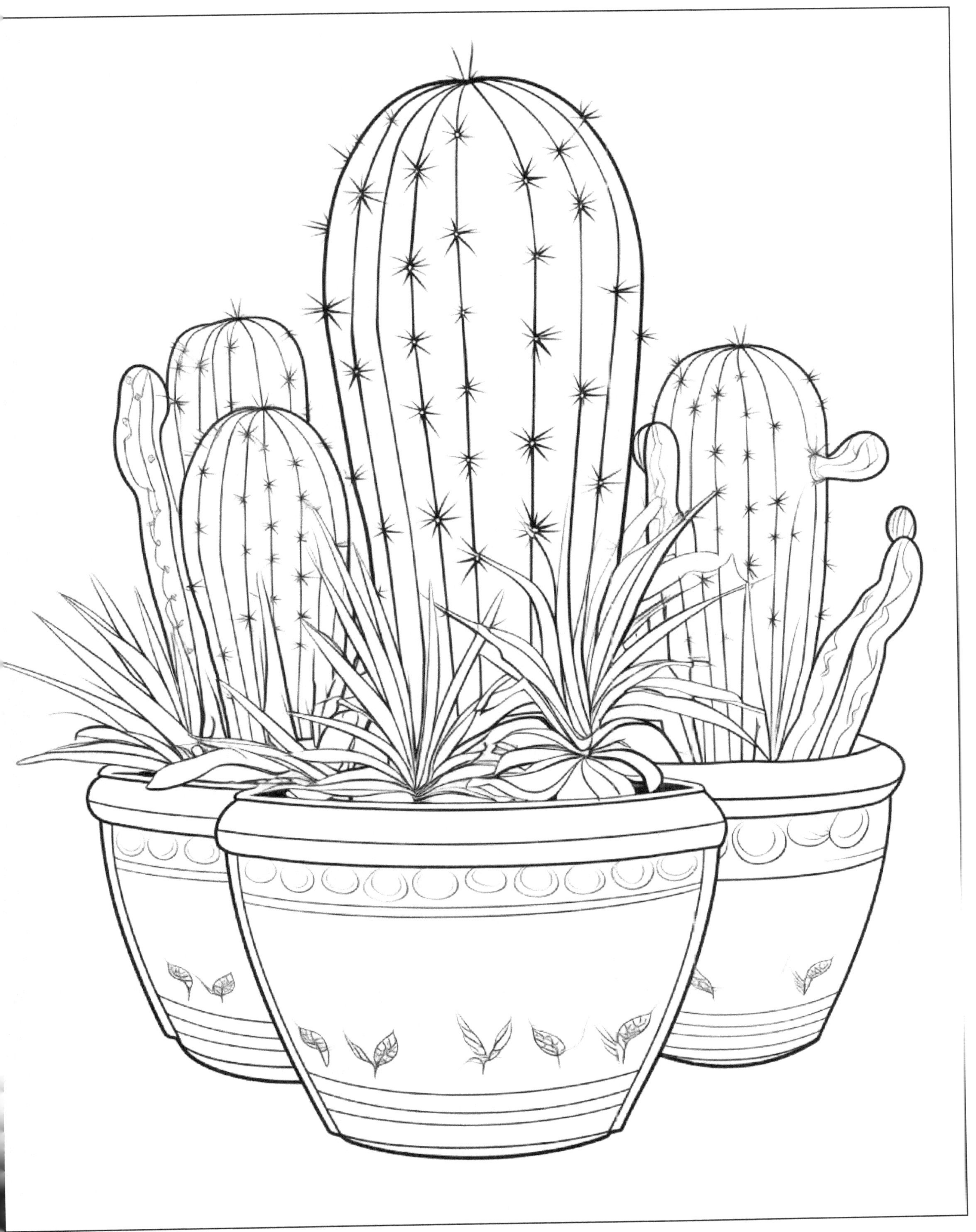

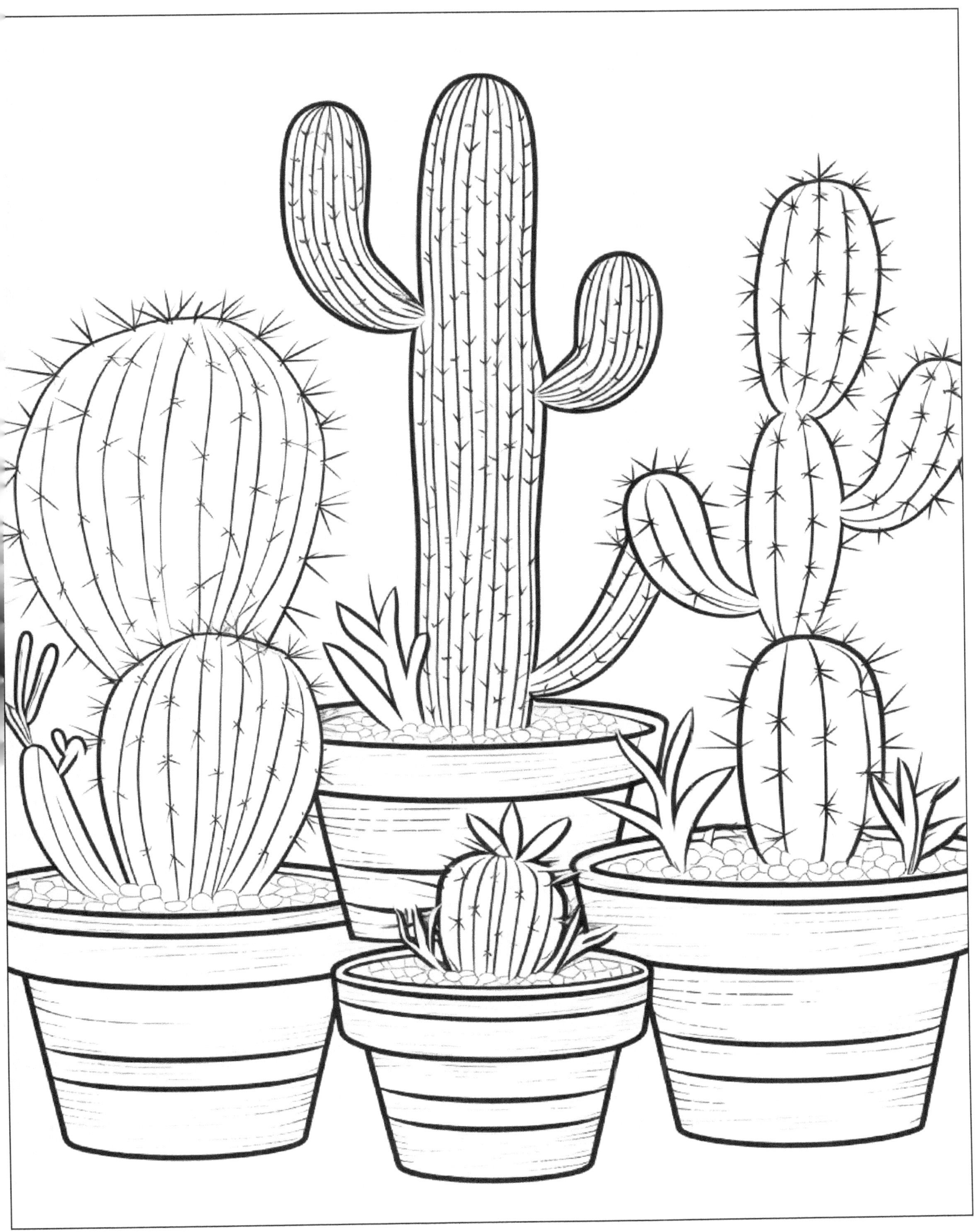

ColorQuest Collections

Fun and creative coloring books for all ages

For more fun and creative coloring books, search for ColorQuest Collections in your favorite bookstore!